i

Car Troubles Causes and Cures

WILLIAM H. CROUSE

Illustrated By
Gene Fleri

Crouse Publishing Company, Inc.
Miami and Naples, Florida

PREFACE

This book is designed to be your guide to solving any problems you have with your automotive vehicle. It describes various possible troubles, their causes, and what must be done to correct the condition.

The book is our attempt to provide you with an easy reference that will help you in your hour of need. It is the outcome of thirty years of studying and writing about automobiles. Our books have been used in many schools in the United States and abroad to train automotive engineers, automotive mechanics, and automotive technicians.

Many people and organizations have helped in the preparation of this book, too numerous to mention in this brief space. Thanks to them all. Special thanks are due to John Steck, professional automotive teacher, adviser, and critic, for his analysis of the manuscript. Special thanks are also due to Gene Fleri, the artist who prepared the illustrations for the book.

Printed in the United States of America
ISBN: 0-911709-00-2 paper

Distributed by William Kaufman, Inc.
Los Altos, CA 94022

CONTENTS

Books By William H. Crouse

Automotive Electronics and Electrical Equipment

Automotive Mechanics

Automotive Service Business

Automotive Engine Design

Books by William H. Crouse and Donald L. Anglin

Automotive Air Conditioning

Automotive Automatic Transmissions

Automotive Manual Transmissions and Power Trains

Automotive Body Repair and Refinishing

Automotive Brakes, Suspension, and Steering

Automotive Emission Control

Automotive Engines

Automotive Fuel, Lubricating, and Cooling Systems

Automotive Technician's Handbook

Automotive Tuneup

General Power Mechanics

Motorcycle Mechanics

Motor Vehicle Inspection

Small Engine Mechanics

The Auto Book

PREFACE

What Car Troubles Will do for You:

CAR TROUBLES gives you *causes* of car troubles.

CAR TROUBLES gives you *cures* for car troubles.

CAR TROUBLES gives you buzz words for the mechanics.

CLUES

For example — Hard starting? What kind? Hard starting cold? Hard starting hot? No cranking? Slow cranking? The books tells all — causes and cures!

BUZZ WORDS

Talk to the mechanic with confidence. Spring the buzz words the book gives you. For example, hard starting with the engine hot. You say, "Must be the choke. Can't be the battery or ignition because the engine starts okay when cold." This gives the mechanic clues that make it possible to locate and fix the trouble quickly. This saves you time and money.

CHAPTER 1
How to Use the Book

First, know your car. What kind of engine does it have? Gasoline or diesel? If gasoline, does it have a carburetor or fuel injection? Drum brakes or disk brakes? Rear-wheel drive or front-wheel drive? All this is important because we divide trouble diagnosis into two or more parts. For example:

Chapter 2
Engine Problems — Gasoline Engine with Carburetor
Chapter 3
Engine Problems — Gasoline Engine with Fuel Injection
Chapter 4
Engine Problems — Automotive Diesel Engines

Suppose you have an engine problem. You go to the chapter that relates to your car's engine (Chap. 2, 3, or 4). Find the section that applies to your problem — *Hard Starting,* for example. There you will find possible causes and cures of your problem.

WHAT'S UNDER THE HOOD

Figure 1-1 shows you major parts under the hood. Open the hood of your car and get acquainted with them. These are the parts you may need to check or work on in case of emergency.

TROUBLE DIAGNOSIS

Finding the cause of a trouble is called *trouble diagno-*

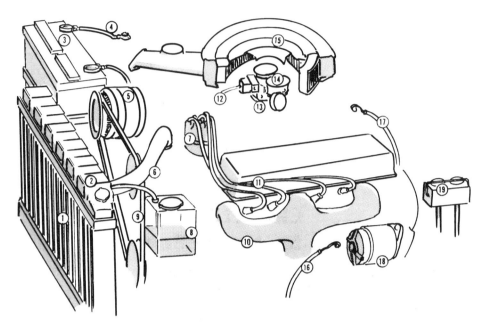

1-1 The important things under the hood that you should become acquainted with: 1. radiator, 2. radiator cap, 3. battery, 4. battery ground cable, 5. alternator, 6. radiator upper hose, 7. distributor, 8. expansion tank, 9. fan belt, 10. manifold, 11. sparkplug cables, 12. 13. 14. carburetor components, 15. air cleaner, 16. starting motor cable, 17. engine ground cable, 18. starting motor, 19. brake master cylinder.

sis, or, in shop talk, *troubleshooting.* Troubleshooting is partly an art, partly a science. The expert automotive technician not only uses his or her brain but may also use testing instruments to pinpoint a trouble cause.

However, anyone who has eyes that can see, and ears that can hear, can do a pretty good job of guestimating just what is causing a problem. What this amounts to is identifying the trouble and then considering the most probable cause as listed on following pages. We look at each kind of trouble you might have, and then list and describe possible causes. Also, we explain how the trouble can be cured.

Note: If the job will take professional help — an automotive technician or mechanic — we indicate this with **Get Help.**

HELPFUL TROUBLE-DIAGNOSIS HINTS

When you have car trouble, ask yourself:

"Did this happen all at once?"

"Did I see it coming on? Was I getting hints that something was going wrong?"

"Did something unusual happen just before I noticed the trouble?"

The answers may lead you to the basic cause. For instance, the car ahead of you suddenly stops and you rear-end it because you can't stop in time. Fortunately, your bumper took the impact without damage to the car. But it was a pretty good bump. A day or two later you try to start and nothing happens. You open the hood and notice that the battery is loose in its holder. Your diagnosis — the bump was hard enough to shift the battery and loosen a connection. Your correction — clean and tighten the battery cables and tighten the battery hold-down clamps (see page 98).

At the same time, ask yourself, "Are the brakes a little weak?" Have you noticed that it takes longer to stop? Maybe you should have the brakes serviced (**Get Help**). Otherwise, the next emergency stop might have a more serious ending.

DON'T TREAT THE SYMPTOMS ONLY

Remember this — don't treat the symptoms and forget to take care of the basic problem. Suppose your battery runs down so you can't start. You get a jump start from the battery in another car (see page 101 on how to safely jump-start). Then you get a battery charge from a service station. You have taken care of the symptom. But why did the battery run down? Was it charging system trouble? A bad battery that can't hold a charge? A slow leak in the electrical system? Whatever it is, you should have it fixed (**Get Help**) so you won't have the same problem again.

YOUR EMERGENCY REPAIR KIT

Figure 1-2 shows a complete emergency kit that equips you for many emergencies you might encounter on the highway. Of course if you drive only around town, and

1-2   Your emergency repair kit.

only in the daytime, you don't need much of an emergency repair kit. Help is just around the corner. But if you hit the highways, day and night, summer and winter, you should have an emergency kit that will help you in time of need.

CHAPTER 2
Engine Problems — Gasoline Engines with Carburetor

Many engine problems are common to all three types of engines — Gasoline Engines with Carburetor, Gasoline Engines with Fuel Injection, Automotive Diesel Engines. But there are special problems that occur in only one of these three. And servicing procedures are somewhat different for the three. That is why we have three separate chapters for the three types of engine. Chapter 1 covers the fundamentals of trouble diagnosis. You should have this general background information in mind when you are trying to pinpoint a problem cause. This chapter covers gasoline engines using a carburetor.

HOW TO FIND THE CAUSE OF YOUR TROUBLE — GASOLINE ENGINE WITH CARBURETOR

Run down the list that follows to find your problem. Under that heading you will find possible causes and cures of the problem.

Technical Explanation

The carburetor (Fig. 1-1) is a mixing device that mixes gasoline vapor with air to make a combustible mixture (Fig. 2-1). This mixture burns in the engine to produce the power that moves the car.

Hard Starting

There are several kinds of "hard starting". Run down

5

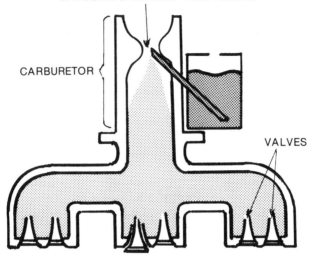

GASOLINE SPRAYING FROM NOZZLE

CARBURETOR

VALVES

2-1   Carburetor and intake manifold. Air flowing toward the engine passes through the carburetor where it picks up gasoline vapor. The mixture flows into the intake manifold and then into the engine cylinders when intake valves open.

the section headings below to find your trouble. Then read that section to see what might be the cause and what will cure the trouble. In some places we give you a checking routine to help you pinpoint the trouble cause.

1. No Cranking

If the engine does not crank when you try to start, turn on the headlights, or open a door so interior light comes on. Then try to start. Note what happens to the light.

   a. *Light stays bright.* This means that the starting circuit or starting motor is at fault (**Get Help**).
   b. *Light dims considerably.* The battery is probably low. Or the starting motor may be jammed. Possibly, the engine itself could be jammed, but this is a serious condition that would not be likely to happen without some previous warning.

Try a jump start (page 101 explains how to safely jump-start your car using the battery from another car). If the engine now starts and runs, probably the battery is low. Recharge the battery and try to find the cause (**Get Help**).

Note: Cold weather puts an added load on a battery.

It takes more current to crank a cold engine. A low battery might not have enough zip to crank a cold engine.

   c. *Light dims slightly.* This is probably due to a faulty starting motor (**Get Help**).
   d. *Light goes out when you try to start.* There is a poor connection in the starting-motor circuit, probably at the battery. Sometimes wiggling the battery cables improves the connection enough to start. You could also have a very low battery that can give you some light, but dies when you try to start.
   e. *No cranking, no lights.* The battery is dead. Or probably there is a bad connection at the battery. If the battery is old, it is probably worn out and you need a new one. If the battery is fairly new, the charging system may be at fault; it is not keeping the battery charged. Or there is an electrical leak that runs the battery down (**Get Help**).

2. Engine Cranks Slowly But Does Not Start

This is probably due to a low battery. Try a jump start (see page 101). If the engine cranks normally and starts, the battery is low. Recharge it and see if the trouble occurs again. If it does occur a short time later, you probably need a new battery. However, the trouble could be in the charging system. It is not keeping the battery charged (**Get Help**).

Note: If the engine cranks slowly when you try to jump-start it, there is probably trouble in the starting motor or in the engine. But, consider: is the battery in the other car up to charge? Try the battery from still another car before you condemn the engine or starting motor. During cold weather, engines are much harder to start; even a good battery may not be able to crank the engine very fast. (See page 86 on cold-weather starting.)

Also: Perhaps the battery is run down from repeated tries to start the engine. In this case the trouble is in the engine, or the fuel or ignition system, as noted in the following section.

7

3. Engine Cranks at Normal Speed But Does Not Start

The trouble could be in the ignition or fuel system. It might be nothing more serious than over-choking and flooding the engine (filling it with an over-rich mixture).

Modern engines with carburetors have automatic chokes (Fig. 2-2). They supply the engine with extra gasoline (a *rich* mixture) during a cold-engine start. Then, after

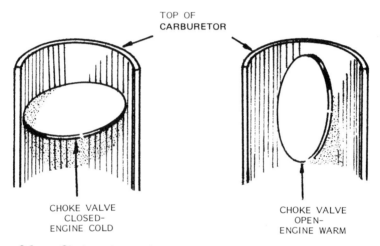

TOP OF
CARBURETOR

CHOKE VALVE
CLOSED-
ENGINE COLD

CHOKE VALVE
OPEN-
ENGINE WARM

2-2 Choke-valve action. When the engine is cold, the choke valve is closed (left) choking off the air flow. When the engine warms up, the choke valve opens (right).

the engine starts, the choke backs off so the engine gets a *leaner* mixture (less gasoline in the air-fuel mixture). If it does not work that way, you could have overchoking (a too-rich mixture) or underchoking (a too-lean mixture) and failure to start.

Technical Explanation

The choke has a round valve located at the top of the carburetor (Fig. 2-2). When the engine is cold, the choke has automatically positioned the valve so it nearly closes off ("chokes") the air flow into the carburetor (left, in Fig. 2-2). Now, when the engine is cranked, it calls for air-fuel mixture. But not much air can get past the choke valve. So, to help satisfy the demand, extra gasoline flows from the fuel nozzle in the carburetor. This produces a rich mixture.

Here's how it works. With the choke nearly closed, choking off the air flow, a partial vacuum develops in the carburetor when the engine is cranked. Atmospheric pressure, working on the gasoline in the carburetor reservoir (the float bowl) pushes gasoline up and out of the fuel nozzle (see Fig. 2-1). After the engine starts, a heat-sensitive device begins to open the choke valve. This leans out the air-fuel mixture. By the time the engine is warmed up, the choke valve is open and air can flow normally through the carburetor.

What to Do

Try starting with the gas pedal pushed down to the floor *and held there* while the engine is cranked, for about ten seconds. If the engine has been *overchoked* and flooded (filled with an over-rich mixture), this will clear the rich mixture away and the engine should start. If it does, the choke may be faulty. If it happens more than once, **Get Help**.

If cranking with the gas pedal held down does not work, the trouble may be underchoking. Try this. Push the gas pedal down to the floor (pump it) several times. This causes the accelerator system in the carburetor to squirt some extra fuel into the intake manifold so the mixture is temporarily enriched. Release the gas pedal and try to start. If the engine now starts, the choke or fuel system is at fault (**Get Help**).

Checking the Choke

You can check the choke by removing the air-cleaner cover (Fig. 1-1). The choke valve should be closed if the engine is cold. It should be open if the engine is hot (Fig. 2-2). If the choke valve is open (engine cold), push it closed and try to start again. But first replace the air-cleaner cover.

Caution: Never try to start the engine with the air-cleaner cover off. If the engine backfires, flames could erupt from the carburetor and ignite gasoline fumes in the engine compartment. This could cause a disastrous fire, and you could be badly burned.

The Spark Test

This is a test that professionals use to find out if the ignition system is working. One lead is disconnected from a spark plug. Figure 2-3 shows how to disconnect a spark-plug cable. Insulated pliers are used to hold the lead clip

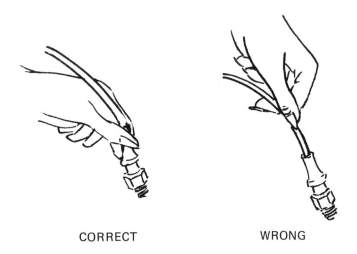

CORRECT   WRONG

2-3   When disconnecting a spark-plug cable, do not pull on the cable. This can damage the cable. Instead, pull on the rubber boot.

about 3/16 inch (5mm) from the engine block (see Fig. 2-4). The engine is then cranked. If a good spark jumps to the block, the ignition system is probably okay. The no-start problem is in the fuel system.

Caution: This test must be done with care because the ignition system can produce 40,000 or more volts and this can give you a bad shock.

Also, the spark-plug cables must be handled carefully. The insulation is soft and if it is damaged, the spark will jump to ground outside the engine and the engine will miss.

Engine Runs But Misses

This means that at least one cylinder is not firing. When a cylinder is not firing, that is, not delivering power,

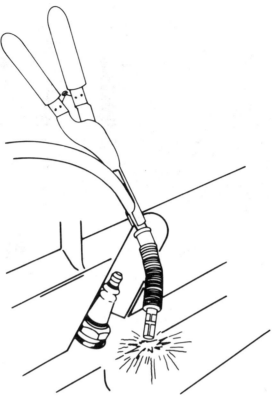

2-4 'To make the spark test, hold the end of the spark-plug cable with insulated pliers close to the engine block. *(Ford Motor Company)*

the engine is thrown out of balance. It runs roughly and lacks full power.

It is sometimes hard to find out which cylinder is missing. The professional uses an oscilloscope (Fig. 2-5) to locate the trouble.

However, the technician may try the elimination test, as follows. With the engine running, use insulated pliers to disconnect and then reconnect each spark-plug cable in turn. Disconnecting a cable keeps the spark from reaching the spark plug. If disconnecting a cable does change engine speed, then that cylinder was firing.

Careful

The elimination test should not be made on engines

2-5 The technician may use the oscilloscope to check the ignition system and engine operation. *(Sun Electric Corporation)*

equipped with some types of electronic ignition systems. It can damage them. The professional refers to the manufacturer's shop manual (Fig. 2-6) before trying this test to see if the manufacturer okays it.

2-6 When in doubt, the technician checks the car manufacturer's shop manual.

Spark Test of Missing Cylinders

The professional may check a missing cylinder, once it has been located, by trying the spark test (Fig. 2-4) as explained on page 10. If no spark occurs, the trouble is in the ignition system **(Get Help)**. If a spark does occur, a good plug is installed, the cable reconnected, and the engine started again. If the engine still misses, the trouble is in the engine, probably due to defective parts such as valves, piston, or piston rings **(Get Help)**.

Engine Lacks Power

In addition to missing, as noted above, other things can cause an engine to lose power. You will need professional help to correct these problems.

1. *Defective ignition.* This can cause missing.

2. *Defective fuel system.* Not enough fuel is being delivered to the engine. Or throttle valve (or valves) in the carburetor are not opening fully because the linkage to the gas pedal is not correctly adjusted.

3. *Restricted exhaust* (Fig 2-7). Did the loss of power happen all at once, just after you backed into a wall or a

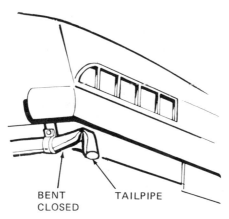

BENT CLOSED   TAILPIPE

2-7 If the tail pipe is bent, it will prevent normal exhaust from the engine, and engine power will be reduced. *(Ford Motor Company)*

high curb? You may have bent the exhaust pipe. Or a collapsed inner layer of a laminated exhaust pipe (Fig. 2-8)

LAMINATED
EXHAUST PIPE

COLLAPSED
INNER LAYER

2-8   Some cars use a laminated exhaust pipe consisting of an inner and outer layer. If the inner layer collapses, it will prevent normal exhaust from the engine and engine power will be reduced. *(ATW)*

could be the cause.

4. *Heavy oil, or wrong gasoline.* (Change to the specified oil and gasoline to see if this improves engine power.)

5. *Transmission problems.* It may not be downshifting when you press the gas pedal to the floor. Also, the torque converter in the transmission may be bad.

6. *Excessive rolling resistance.* This may rob the engine of enough power so that you blame the engine. But the trouble could be due to low tires, dragging brakes, or wheel misalignment.

7. *Internal engine problems.* Defective or worn parts, or accumulations of carbon may contribute to engine problems.

8. *Overheating engine.* See *Engine Overheats,* below.

Engine Lacks Power Only When Hot

This could be due to a choke that is stuck partly closed. With the engine warmed up, and *turned off,* remove the air-cleaner cover to check the position of the choke valve. If it is partly closed, you need professional help. The choke is defective or misadjusted.

Note: An overheating engine can also cause a loss of power. See *Engine Overheats, below.*

ENGINE OVERHEATS

The temperature gauge or the red temperature light will warn you if the engine is overheating. If the gauge reads in the red danger area, or if the warning light comes on, *pull off the road at once to a safe place, and stop.* If you continue to drive your risk radiator boil-over (steam erupting from your radiator) and serious damage to the engine. Open the hood immediately to let engine heat escape.

Four things can cause engine overheating:

1. *A loose or broken fan belt* (pages 15 to 16).

2. *Loss of coolant* (water) from the engine cooling system (pages 16 to 17).

3. *Driving* in slow-moving traffic on a hot day (page 19).

4. *Engine trouble.*

LOOSE FAN BELT

If the fan belt becomes worn or so loose that it slips and cannot drive the engine fan and water pump fast enough, the engine will overheat. You can check for a loose fan belt by *turning the engine off* and then pressing a thumb against the belt (Fig. 2-9). *Be careful — if the belt has been slipping it will be hot!*

Caution: The engine must be *off* when you test the belt! You could be seriously hurt if you touched the belt when the engine is running.

If you can push the belt in more than 1/2 inch, it is loose. It can be tightened by loosening the alternator brace and pulling out on the alternator while retightening the brace. Have the belt and tension checked at the next service station you come to.

Note: A loose fan belt will sometimes make a squealing noise when you suddenly step on the gas. This happens when the engine picks up speed and there is a

moment's lag during which the belt slips and squeals
before it reaches engine speed.

BROKEN FAN BELT

If the fan belt breaks, you know it at once because the
alternator stops charging. This causes the alternator light
to come on, or the ammeter to show discharge. Without
the belt, the engine fan and water pump stop and the engine overheats in a few minutes. See *Replacing a Broken
Fan Belt* on pages 18 to 19 for what to do.

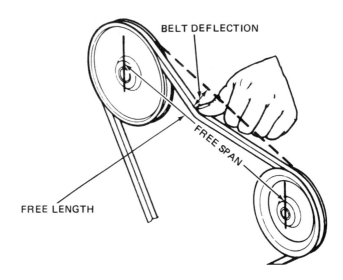

2-9   Checking belt deflection. *(Chrysler Corporation)*

CHECKING COOLANT LEVEL

If the cooling system has an expansion tank (Fig. 2-10),
you can readily see whether the coolant level is low. Otherwise, you will have to remove the radiator cap.

Caution: Never try to check the coolant level in the
radiator if the engine is hot. The cooling system is
pressurized. If you take the radiator cap off you release the pressure, and a burst of steam and scalding
water will erupt from the radiator. This could burn
you seriously.

When the engine has cooled enough for you to hold your hand on the radiator cap, remove the cap to check the coolant level in the radiator. It should be up near the filler tube. If the coolant level is low, look for signs of leaks in your radiator or heater hoses, or in the radiator. Antifreeze has dye in it to make leak detection easier. If you find a leak, you can usually make a temporary repair, as explained on page 19, *Cooling System Temporary Repairs*.

If you see no signs of leaks, and the coolant level is more or less normal, perhaps the driving conditions have caused overheating. Driving in slow-moving traffic on a hot day can cause overheating. See *Hot-Weather Driving Hints* on page 19 for what to do.

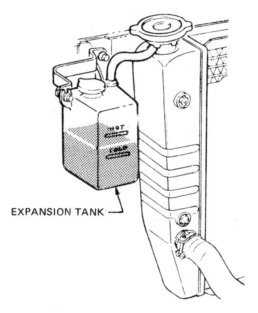

2-10 Expansion tank in a cooling system. *(Ford Motor Company)*

ENGINE TROUBLE

If the overheating is not due to loss of coolant, a slipping or broken belt, or unusual driving conditions, you may have internal engine trouble. It could be that the engine has lost oil, or it has some internal damage. **(Get Help)**.

Replacing a Broken Fan Belt

If the fan belt breaks, the engine will overheat. This belt drives the alternator and radiator fan and water pump (see Fig. 1-1). If the fan and water pump do not work, the engine quickly overheats. You should have a spare fan belt in your emergency kit (two matched belts if the engine uses two). See Figure 1-2. You have three alternatives for replacing the belt:

1. *Wait for the tow truck.* The mechanic can install the new fan belt (or belts).

2. *Drive to the nearest service station.* But first let the engine cool, then fill the radiator or expansion tank to the *full* level. Close the hood. Drive on slowly until the gauge or light signals overheating. Stop, open the hood, and repeat the procedure. Continue this way until you can limp into a service station to have the belt installed.

3. *Install the belt yourself.* The fan belt usually drives the alternator as well as the water pump and radiator fan (Fig. 1-1). In most cars the alternator has an adjustment; a brace that can be loosened so the alternator can be pivoted inward. This allows you to install the belt. Now pivot the alternator outward to put tension on the belt. Tighten the brace. Stop at the next service station and have the attendant check the belt and belt tension.

Caution: Keep your hands and any dangling jewelry or loose clothing away from the fan belt or fan when the engine is running. The moving fan or fan belt can hurt you badly. On many cars with the engine mounted sideways (transversally), the radiator fan is driven by an electric motor (Fig. 2-11). This motor can turn on without warning if the engine is warm and not running. Professionals disconnect the fan before working under the hood.

COOLING SYSTEM TEMPORARY REPAIR

After the engine has cooled, add water to the expansion tank or radiator as necessary to replace coolant that was lost. Then make temporary repairs of leaks, as follows.

A leak under a hose clamp may sometimes be fixed by tightening the clamp with a screwdriver. If the leak is in a hose, wrap it with tape from your emergency repair kit

(Fig. 1-2). Replace the radiator cap but do not tighten it. If you tighten the cap, the system will pressurize and the leak could open up again. Drive slowly to the nearest service station to have the hose or clamp replaced.

Have the coolant checked for antifreeze protection. Add antifreeze as necessary to restore protection to the lowest temperature you expect to meet.

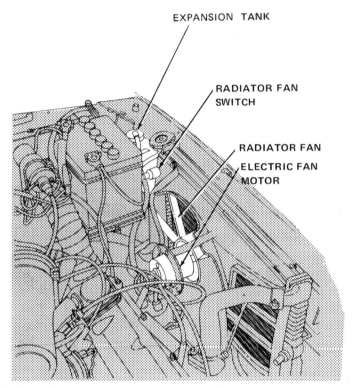

EXPANSION TANK

RADIATOR FAN SWITCH

RADIATOR FAN

ELECTRIC FAN MOTOR

2-11   Many late-model cars have the engine mounted sideways, or transversally. The radiator fan mounts at the front, back of the radiator, and is driven by an electric motor. *(Chrysler Corporation)*.

Hot-Weather Driving Hint

If you are stuck in slow-moving traffic on a hot day, the engine may start to overheat. You can help by (1) opening the car windows, (2) turning off the air conditioner and (3) turning on the car heater. These three steps lighten the load on the engine cooling system and drain away some of the heat from the engine. *You* will be uncomfortable, but this procedure may make the difference between only a hot engine, and an overheated engine with radiator boil-over and possible engine damage.

Vapor Lock

Sometimes the fuel pump will get so hot that the gasoline in it will vaporize. This causes *vapor lock,* which keeps gasoline from getting to the carburetor. The engine stalls. If this is the problem, wait a while for the engine to cool and the vapor lock will disappear so you can get on your way again.

ENGINE IDLES ROUGHLY

This could be due to an incorrect carburetor idle adjustment or to trouble in one of the emission-control systems on the engine. It could also be due to problems described above under *Engine Lacks Power* (**Get Help**).

ENGINE STARTS AND THEN STALLS

If the engine starts properly when cold and then stalls as it warms up, the choke valve may be stuck closed. This causes the engine to get an over-rich mixture so it stalls as it warms up. (See *Checking the Choke* page 9.) Other possible causes could be overheated engine, vapor lock, improperly set idle, or trouble in one of the emission-control systems (**Get Help**).

ENGINE BACKFIRES

You need professional help. The problem could come from incorrect ignition timing, wrong spark plugs, too rich or lean air-fuel mixture, carbon in the engine, or internal engine problems such as hot or stuck valves.

ENGINE RUN-ON, OR DIESELING

With this condition, the engine attempts to continue running after the ignition is turned off. Air-fuel mixture is leaking past the throttle valve and hot spots in the engine cylinders act like spark plugs, causing the cylinders to fire. This can damage the engine and it should be corrected without delay (**Get Help**).

Possible causes include incorrect idle-stop adjustment, overheated engine, ignition timing advanced, and trouble in the engine. If your engine diesels, apply the foot brake hard and shift into gear. This will stall the engine (**Get Help**).

SMOKY EXHAUST

Technicians classify smoky exhaust as (1) Blue Smoke, (2) Black Smoke, or (3) White Smoke. Here is what each means.

1. *Blue Smoke*. This means that the engine is burning lubricating oil. Usually the cause is worn engine parts that allow lubricating oil to work its way up into the engine cylinders, where it is burned. The remedy is an engine overhaul (**Get Help**).

2. *Black Smoke*. This means an excessively rich air-fuel mixture. There is so much gasoline in the mixture that it is only partly burned and black smoke results. This can be caused by defects in the ignition or fuel system, or in the engine itself (**Get Help**).

3. *White Smoke*. This is steam. Coolant is leaking into the engine cylinders where it turns into steam. Residue from the antifreeze can gum valves and piston rings and cause serious engine trouble. Replace gaskets and tighten cylinder-head bolts to eliminate the leakage (**Get Help**).

EXCESSIVE OIL CONSUMPTION

If you have to add oil to the engine frequently, or if the exhaust is blue, chances are you have an older, high-mileage engine. Cylinder walls and valve guides are probably worn, so oil gets up into the cylinders where it is burned. This causes blue smoke. High oil consumption could also result from oil leaks from the engine. Check the surface under your car where it is normally parked. If you see oil, there is leakage (**Get Help**).

EXCESSIVE FUEL CONSUMPTION

This can result from many conditions, from the drivers style of driving to defects in the engine or drive train. A driver who nervously pumps the gas pedal and jack-rabbits away when the light changes to green is going to burn extra fuel. The person who habitually drives fast, or who takes only short trips around town, is also going to get poor gasoline mileage.

Problems in the carburetor can cause excessive fuel consumption. Sometimes the ignition system may be the cause. A worn engine requires more fuel to produce normal power **(Get Help)**.

ENGINE NOISES

The engine can make a variety of noises, some that are unimportant, and others that signal something may be wrong **(Get Help)**.

1. *Valve and tappet noise.* This is a regular clicking noise that sometimes disappears at high speeds. It is caused by excessive clearance in the valve trains. Some slight valve and tappet noise is acceptable, but if it is excessive, correction must be made.

2. *Pinging.* This is a metallic chattering noise that becomes noticeable during acceleration, or when climbing a hill. It is sometimes called "spark knock", and is due to the detonation of the last part of the charges of air-fuel mixture that are burned in the engine cylinders. This action can damage the engine. Sometimes it can be cured by using a higher-octane fuel. If pinging continues, you may need an engine job. It could be due to carbon accumulations in the engine, or to the wrong ignition timing.

3. *Squeal.* This is probably due to a loose fan belt. The belt slips and there is high-pitched squealing noises when the engine speed is suddenly increased. See *Loose Fan Belt,* pages 15 to 16.

Other noises that result from wear or damage and that may require engine servicing are:

    a. *Connecting rod* noises which are most noticeable when the engine is "floating" — neither accelerating nor decelerating. It is a light knocking or pounding noise.

    b. *Piston-pin* noise which sounds somewhat like valve-and-tappet noise, but it has a unique metallic double knock.

c. *Piston-ring* noise is more of a clicking, snapping, or rattling sound. It is usually due to broken rings.

d. *Piston slap* is a muffled, hollow, bell-like noise. It results from worn cylinder walls or pistons.

e. *Crankshaft knock* is a heavy, dull, metallic knock, most noticeable when the engine is under heavy load, or accelerating. It is usually due to worn bearings.

4. *Miscellaneous noises.* Anything that is loose in the engine compartment can cause noise — alternator, starting motor, horn, water pump, manifolds, oil pan, and so on.

CHAPTER 3
Engine Problems — Gasoline Engine with Fuel Injection

Many engine problems are common to all three types of engines — Gasoline Engines with Carburetor, Gasoline Engines with Fuel Injection, Automotive Diesel Engines. But there are special problems that occur in only one of these three. And servicing procedures are somewhat different for the three. That is why we have three separate chapters for the three types of engines. Chapter 1 covers the fundamentals of trouble diagnosis. You should have this general background information in mind when you are trying to pinpoint a problem cause. This chapter covers gasoline engines using fuel injection.

TYPES OF FUEL INJECTION SYSTEMS

Gasoline engines use two basic types of fuel injection. The difference is in where the fuel is injected. In one type, the fuel is injected (or sprayed) into the throttle body (Fig. 3-1). It mixes with the air moving into the intake manifold to form a combustible mixture. The throttle body (Fig. 3-2) is the lower part of the carburetor which contains the throttle valve (or valves). With this arrangement, the upper part of the carburetor has been discarded and replaced by a fuel injector valve. This valve is much like the nozzle on a garden hose (Fig. 3-3). When you turn the hose nozzle, you can let the water spray out, or you can shut it off. In the same way, the fuel injector valve can be opened to spray

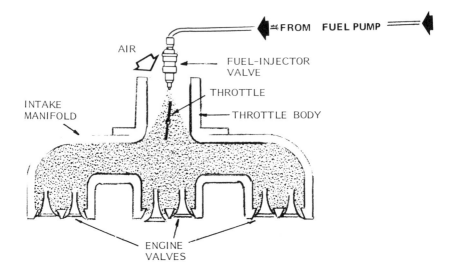

3-1   The throttle-body fuel-injection system has the fuel-injection valve located in the throttle body. When activated by the electronic control system, it sprays gasoline into the intake manifold, as shown. Notice that the throttle is open.

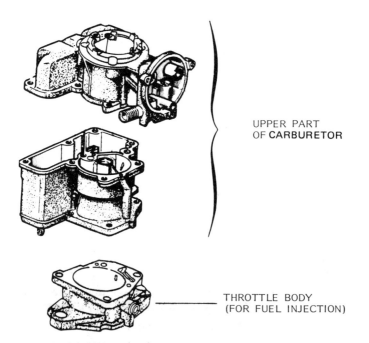

3-2   The throttle body is the lower part of the carburetor. With throttle-body fuel injection, the upper parts of the carburetor are replaced with the fuel-injection valve.

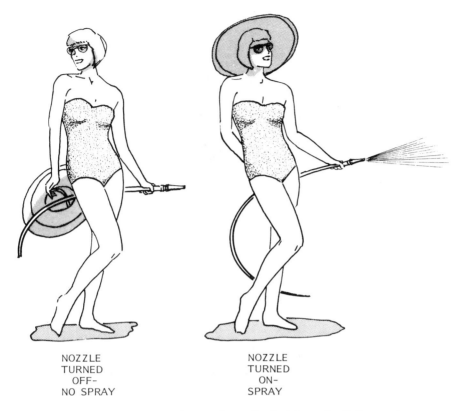

NOZZLE
TURNED
OFF—
NO SPRAY

NOZZLE
TURNED
ON—
SPRAY

3-3 The hose nozzle can be adjusted to cut off the water spray, or allow water to spray out.

fuel, or shut to stop the flow of fuel. When it is time for the fuel injector valve to spray fuel, the electronic control system opens the valve. When the proper amount of fuel has been sprayed out, the electronic control system shuts the valve.

The electronic control system receives signals from the engine — throttle position, engine temperature, air-fuel mixture richness, and so on. It puts these together and "decides" how long to hold the fuel injector valve open. For acceleration, higher speed, and greater power demand, it holds the valve open longer. More fuel is sprayed.

The second type of fuel injection has one fuel injector valve for each engine cylinder (Fig. 3-4). In this system, the valves are located in the intake manifold, opposite the intake valves. Just before an intake valve opens, the fuel in-

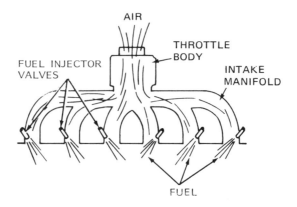

AIR

THROTTLE
BODY

FUEL INJECTOR
VALVES

INTAKE
MANIFOLD

FUEL

3-4   Some gasoline fuel-injection systems have fuel-injection valves inside the intake manifold, just opposite the intake valves. There is one fuel-injection valve for each engine cylinder.

jector valve opens to spray fuel into the air in the manifold. When the intake valve opens, this fuel, mixed with air, enters the engine cylinder. Here again, the length of time the injector valve is open and the amount of fuel sprayed is determined by the electronic control system. It depends on operating and engine conditions.

Note: The fuel-injection systems described above are called intermittent, or timed, systems. The injection valves are the off-on type. That is, they open only at the right moment as required by the engine cylinders. There is also the continuous-injection type. In this type, the injection valve is open and spraying continuously. The system measures the amount of air going to the engine cylinders and adjusts the fuel flow so that the air-fuel mixture is correct.

HOW TO FIND THE CAUSE OF YOUR TROUBLE — GASOLINE ENGINE WITH FUEL INJECTION

Listed below are various problems for gasoline engines using fuel injection. The list includes *Hard Starting, Engine Misses, Engine Lacks Power, Engine Overheats,* and so on. Run down the list to find your problem. Then note the possible causes. For example, the first trouble is *hard starting.* Notice the different kinds of hard starting. Pick the one that applies.

HARD STARTING

There are several kinds of "Hard Starting". Run down the section headings below to find your trouble. Then read that section to see what might be the cause and what will cure the trouble. In some places we give you a checking routine which will help you pinpoint the trouble cause.

1. No Cranking

If the engine does not crank when you try to start, turn on the headlights, or open a door so an interior light comes on. Then try to start. Note what happens to the light.

    a. *Light stays bright.* This means that the starting circuit or starting motor is at fault **(Get Help)**.

    b. *Light dims considerably.* The battery is probably low. Or the starting motor may be jammed. Possibly, the engine itself could be jammed, but this is a serious condition that would not be apt to happen without some previous warning.

Try a jump start (page 101). If the engine now starts and runs, probably the battery is low. Recharge the battery and try to find the cause **(Get Help)**.

Note: Cold weather puts an added load on a battery. It takes more current to crank a cold engine. A low battery might not have enough zip to crank a cold engine.

    c. *Light dims slightly.* This is probably due to a faulty starting motor **(Get Help)**.

    d. *Light goes out when you try to start.* There is a poor connection in the starting-motor circuit, probably at the battery. Sometimes wiggling the battery cables improves the connection enough to start. The remedy is to clean and tighten the connection (page 98, or **Get Help**). You could also have a very low battery that can give you some light, but dies when you try to start.

    e. *No cranking, no lights.* The battery is dead. Or possibly there is a bad connection at the battery. If the battery is old, it is probably worn out and you need a new one. If the battery is fairly new, the charging system may be at fault. It is not keeping the battery charged. Or there is an electrical leak that runs the battery down **(Get Help)**.

2. Engine Cranks Slowly But Does Not Start

This is probably due to a low battery. Try a jump start (see page 101). If the engine then cranks normally and starts, your battery is low. Recharge it and see if the trouble occurs again. If it does happen again a short time later, you probably need a new battery. However, the trouble could be in the charging system. It is not keeping the battery charged **(Get Help)**.

Note: If the engine cranks slowly when you try to jump-start it, there is probably trouble in the starting motor or in the engine. But consider this: "Is the battery in the *other* car up to charge?" Try the battery from still another car before you condemn the engine or starting motor. During cold weather, engines are much harder to start. Even a good battery may not be able to crank the engine very fast. (See page 86 for cold-weather starting.)

Also: Perhaps the battery is run down from repeated tries at starting the engine. In this case, the trouble could be in the engine or the fuel or ignition system as noted in the following section.

3. Engine Cranks at Normal Speed But Does Not Start

The trouble could be in the ignition or fuel system. It might be nothing more serious than flooding the engine (filling it with an over-rich mixture). Push the gas pedal to the floor and try to start. If the engine now starts and runs, that may be all that was wrong. If the trouble occurs again, get professional help. There is probably a leaky fuel injection valve, or some problem in the electronic control system that is sending the wrong signals to the fuel-injector valves.

Note: Many modern electronic fuel-injection systems can self-diagnose any problems that occur. That is, if a trouble starts to develop, a dash *Check Engine* light will come on to tell the driver that something is wrong. The system meantime stores a code which will identify the problem area. This helps the technician locate the trouble spot so repairs can be made.

If the engine does not start when you crank with the gas pedal pushed down, you have either fuel-system or ignition-system trouble. It is going to take professional help to find the cause and correct it.

The Spark Test

Professionals sometimes use the spark test to see if the ignition system is working. This is done by disconnecting a spark-plug cable and holding the lead clip close to the engine block (Fig. 2-4). Then the engine is cranked to see if a good spark will jump to the block. If it does, the ignition system is probably okay. (See *The Spark Test,* page 10, which explains how to make this test.)

Note: Some engines, when they get very hot, will not start easily until they have cooled off a little. For example, after a hard run in hot weather, and then parking even briefly in the sun, vapor lock can form in the fuel line. That is, the fuel has vaporized and formed a vapor bubble. This prevents delivery of fuel to the engine, so it cannot start. One way to avoid this problem is to park in a shady spot and then open the hood of the car to let the heat escape. If the problem persists, get professional help.

ENGINE RUNS BUT MISSES

This means that one or more cylinders is not firing. When a cylinder is not firing that is, not delivering power — the engine is thrown out of balance. It runs roughly and lacks full power. It is sometimes hard to find out which cylinder is missing. The professional technician uses an oscilloscope (Fig. 2-5) to locate the trouble.

However, the technician may try the elimination test, as follows. With the engine running, use insulated pliers to disconnect, and then reconnect, each spark-plug cable in turn, one at a time. Figure 2-3 shows how to disconnect a spark-plug cable. Disconnecting a cable keeps the spark from reaching the spark plug so the cylinder does not fire. If disconnecting a cable does not change the engine speed, then you have found the missing cylinder. That cylinder was not delivering power before you disconnected the cable. If disconnecting a cable does change engine speed, then that cylinder was firing.

Careful! This test should not be made on engines equipped with some types of electronic ignition systems. It can damage them. The professional refers to the manufacturer's shop manual (Fig. 2-6) before trying this test to see if the manufacturer okays it.

The professional may check a missing cylinder, once it has been located, by trying the spark test (Fig. 2-4) as explained on page 10. If no spark occurs, the trouble is in the ignition system. If a spark does occur, a good spark plug is installed and the engine again started. If the engine still misses, the trouble is in the engine, probably due to defective parts such as valves, piston, or piston rings **(Get Help)**.

ENGINE LACKS POWER

In addition to missing, as noted above, other things can cause an engine to lose power. You will need professional help to correct these problems.

1. *Defective ignition.* This causes missing (described above).
2. *Defective fuel system.* Not enough fuel is being delivered to the engine. This could result from a defective fuel pump, a clogged fuel line or filter, or a defective fuel-pressure regulator.
3. *Defective electronic control system.* The wrong signals are being sent to the fuel or ignition system.
4. *Restricted exhaust* (Fig. 2-7). Did the loss of power happen all at once, just after you backed into a wall, on a high curb? You may have bent the exhaust pipe. This prevents normal engine exhaust and cuts down engine power. Or a collapsed inner layer of a laminated exhaust pipe (Fig. 2-8) could be the cause. In either case, **Get Help.**
5. *Heavy oil, or wrong gasoline.* Change to the specified oil and gasoline to see if this improves engine power.
6. *Transmission problems.* It may not be downshifting

when you press the gas pedal to the floor. Also, the torque converter in the transmission may be bad.

7. *Rolling resistance.* This may rob the engine of enough power so that you blame the engine. But the trouble could be due to low tires, dragging brakes, or wheel misalignment.

8. *Internal engine problems.* These may include defective or worn parts, or accumulation of carbon.

9. *Overheating engine.* See *Engine Overheats,* below.

ENGINE OVERHEATS

The temperature gauge or the red temperature light will warn you if the engine is overheating. If the gauge reads in the red danger area, or if the warning light comes on, pull over to a safe place and stop! If you continue to drive, you risk radiator boil-over (steam erupting from the radiator) and serious damage to the engine. Open the hood to let engine heat escape.

Four things can cause engine overheating:

1. *A loose or broken fan belt* (pages 15 to 16).

2. *Loss of coolant* (water) from the engine cooling system (pages 16 to 17).

3. *Driving* in slow-moving traffic on a hot day (page 19).

4. *Engine trouble.*

LOOSE FAN BELT

If the fan belt (Fig. 1-1) becomes worn or loose so that it slips and cannot drive the engine fan and water pump fast enough, the engine will overheat. You can check for a loose fan belt by *turning the engine off* and then pressing a thumb against the belt (Fig 2-9). Be careful — if the belt has been slipping it will be hot!

Caution: The engine must be *off* when you test the belt. You could be seriously hurt if you touched the belt when the engine was running.

If you can push the belt in more than a half-inch, it is loose. It can be tightened by loosening the alternator brace and pulling out on the alternator while retightening the brace. Have the belt and tension checked at the nearest service station.

Note: A loose fan belt will sometimes make a squealing noise when you suddenly step on the gas. This happens when the engine picks up speed and there is a moment's lag, during which the belt slips and squeals before it reaches engine speed.

BROKEN FAN BELT

If the fan belt (Fig. 1-1) breaks, you know it at once because the alternator stops charging. This causes the alternator light to come on, or the ammeter to show discharge. Without the belt, the engine fan and water pump stop and the engine overheats in a few minutes. See *Replacing a Broken Fan Belt* on pages 18 to 19 for what to do.

Caution: Keep your hands and any dangling jewelry or loose clothing away from the fan belt and fan when the engine is running. The moving fan or fan belt can hurt you badly. Also, some transversally-mounted engines (engines mounted sideways) have electric motor-driven fans (Fig. 2-11). The fan motor can turn on without warning with the engine warm and not running. Professionals disconnect the fan before working under the hood.

CHECKING COOLANT LEVEL

If the cooling system has an expansion tank (Fig. 2-10), you can readily see if the coolant level is low. Otherwise, you will have to remove the radiator cap.

Caution: Never try to check the coolant level in the radiator if the engine is hot. The cooling system is pressurized. If you take the radiator cap off when the engine is hot, you release the pressure and a burst of steam and scalding water will erupt from the radiator. This could burn you seriously.

When the engine has cooled enough for you to hold your hand on the radiator cap, remove the cap and check the coolant level in the radiator. It should be up near the filler tube. If the coolant level is low, look for signs of leaks in your radiator or radiator hose. Antifreeze has dye in it to make leak detection easier. If you find a leak, you can usually make a temporary repair as explained on page 19, *Cooling System Temporary Repairs*.

If you see no signs of leaks, and the coolant level is close to normal, perhaps the driving conditions have caused overheating. See *Hot-Weather Driving Hints* on page 20 for what to do.

ENGINE TROUBLES

If the overheating is not due to loss of coolant, a slipping or broken fan belt, or unusual driving conditions, you may have internal engine trouble. It could be that the engine has lost oil, or it has some internal damage. **Get Help.**

ENGINE IDLES ROUGHLY

This could be due to the electronic control unit giving the wrong signal to the fuel system so that too much fuel is delivered during idle. The trouble may also be due to a malfunctioning pressure regulator, an injection valve that does not close, or to one of the sensing devices in the system that is reporting incorrect information to the electronic control unit. For instance, if the temperature sensor reports that the engine temperature is low, even though it is high, the control unit will operate in the cold-engine mode. That is, it will send extra fuel to the engine (**Get Help**).

ENGINE STARTS AND THEN STALLS

You need professional help. The cause could be engine overheating, vapor lock, or troubles in the electronic system, fuel system, or ignition system.

ENGINE BACKFIRES

You need professional help. The problem could come from incorrect ignition timing, wrong spark plug, an air-fuel mixture that is too lean or too rich, carbon accumulation in the engine, or internal engine problems such as hot or stuck valves.

ENGINE RUN-ON, OR DIESELING

With this condition, the engine attempts to continue running — after the ignition is turned off. Fuel is getting to the engine and hot spots in the engine are acting like spark plugs, causing the cylinders to fire. This can be very damaging to the engine and it should be corrected without delay.

Note: If your engine diesels, apply the foot brake hard and shift into gear. This will stall the engine (**Get Help**).

SMOKY EXHAUST

Technicians classify smoky exhaust as (1) *Blue Smoke,* (2) *Black Smoke,* or (3) *White Smoke.* Here is what each means:

1. *Blue Smoke:* This means that the engine is burning oil. Usually the cause is worn engine parts that allow lubricating oil to work its way into the engine cylinders, where it is burned. The remedy is an engine overhaul (**Get Help**).

2. *Black Smoke:* This signals an excessively rich air-fuel mixture. There is so much gasoline in the mixture that it is only partly burned and black smoke results. This can be caused by defects in the ignition or fuel system, in the electronic control system, or in the engine itself (**Get Help**).

3. *White Smoke:* This is steam. Coolant is leaking into the engine cylinders where it turns into steam. Residue from the antifreeze can gum valves and piston rings and cause serious engine trouble. Replace gaskets and tighten cylinder-heat bolts to eliminate the leakage (**Get Help**).

EXCESSIVE OIL CONSUMPTION

If you have to add oil to the engine frequently, or the exhaust is blue, chances are you have an older, high-mileage engine. Cylinder walls and valve guides are probably worn, so excessive oil gets up into the cylinder where it is burned. The exhaust will be blue. The excessive oil consumption could also be due to oil leaks from the engine. Check the surface under your car where it is normally parked. If you see oil, there is leakage (**Get Help**).

EXCESSIVE FUEL CONSUMPTION

This can result from many conditions, from the drivers style of driving to defects in the engine or drive train. A driver who floors the gas pedal and jack-rabbits away when the light changes to green, and drives at high speed, is going to burn extra fuel. The person who takes short trips around town is going to get poor gasoline mileage.

Problems in the fuel or ignition system, or the electronic control system, can cause poor gasoline mileage. Any condition that causes poor engine performance or engine missing is going to increase fuel consumption. Fuel consumption will increase if the tires are low, if brakes are dragging, wheels are misaligned, or there are problems in the transmission and drive train. As you can see, if the low gasoline mileage is not the result of driving habits, professional help is needed to correct the problem.

ENGINE NOISES

The engine can make various noises, some that are unimportant, and others that signal something may be wrong. On pages 22 to 23 you will find a list of possible engine noises and what could cause them.

CHAPTER 4
Engine Problems —
Automotive Diesel Engines

Many engine problems are common to all three types of engines: Gasoline Engines with Carburetor, Gasoline Engines with Fuel Injection, Automotive Diesel Engines. But there are special problems that occur in only one of these three. And servicing procedures are somewhat different for the three. That is why we have three separate chapters for the three types of engines.

Chapter 1 covers the fundamentals of trouble diagnosis. You should have this general background information in mind when you are trying to pinpoint a problem cause. This chapter (Chapter 4) covers automotive diesel engines.

DIESEL ENGINE OPERATION

In gasoline engines, the fuel is mixed with air outside of the engine. The mixture is then drawn into the engine and burned to produce engine power. In the diesel engine, the fuel is mixed with air *inside* the engine. That is, the fuel-injection valves are located inside the engine cylinders (Fig. 4-1). At the right moment each valve opens momentarily to inject (spray) fuel into the air. Air alone is compressed in the diesel-engine cylinders. As the air is compressed, it gets very hot. The air temperature can reach 1000°F (538°C). This high temperature ignites the fuel when it is sprayed into the hot compressed air. The action is called "compression ignition".

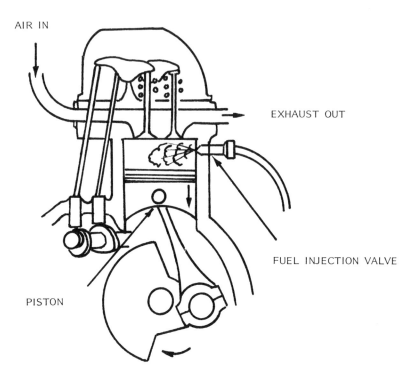

AIR IN

EXHAUST OUT

FUEL INJECTION VALVE

PISTON

4-1 In the diesel engine, the fuel-injection valve is inside the engine cylinder. It injects fuel into the cylinder as the piston nears the top on the compression stroke, compressing the air in the cylinder.

The gasoline engine is called a "spark-ignition" engine because an electric spark ignites the compressed air-fuel mixture. This is actually the basic difference between the two engines, "spark ignition" or "compression ignition". That is, the basic difference is in the way the air-fuel mixture is ignited. The diesel engine uses a different kind of fuel — a light oil. Also, because the pressures inside the engine are higher in the diesel engine, this engine is more heavily constructed.

HOW TO FIND THE CAUSE OF YOUR TROUBLE — AUTOMOTIVE DIESEL ENGINE

Listed below are possible automotive diesel-engine problems. The list includes *Hard Starting, Engine Misses, En-*

gine Lacks Power, Engine Overheats, and so on. Run down the list to find your problem. Then note the possible causes. For example, the first trouble listed is *Hard Starting.* Notice the different kinds of hard starting. Pick the one that applies.

HARD STARTING

There are several kinds of "Hard Starting". Run down the section headings below to find your trouble. Then read that section to see what might be the cause and what will cure the trouble. In some places we give you a checking routine which will help you pinpoint the cause of trouble.

1. No Cranking

If the engine does not crank when you try to start, turn on the headlights, or open a door so an interior light comes on. Then try to start. Notice what happens to the light.

 a. *Light stays bright.* This means that the starting circuit or starting motor is at fault **(Get Help)**.
 b. *Light dims considerably.* The battery is probably low. Or the starting motor may be jammed. Possibly, the engine itself could be jammed, but this is a serious condition that would not be apt to occur without some prior warning.

Try a jump start (see page 101). If the engine now starts and runs, probably your battery is low. Recharge the battery and try to find the cause **(Get Help)**.

Note: Cold weather puts an added load on a battery. It takes more current to crank a cold engine. A low battery might not have enough zip to crank a cold engine.

 c. *Light barely dims.* This is probably due to a faulty starting motor **(Get Help)**.
 d. *Light goes out when you try to start.* There is a poor connection in the starting-motor circuit, probably at the battery. Sometimes wiggling the battery cables improves the connection enough to start. The remedy is to clean and tighten the connection (page 98 or **Get Help**). You could also have a very low battery which can give you some light, but dies

41

when you try to start.

e. *No cranking, no lights.* The battery is dead. Or possibly there is a bad connection at the battery. If the battery is old, it is probably worn out and you need a new one. If the battery is relatively new, the charging system may be at fault in not keeping the battery charged. Or there is an electrical leak that runs the battery down (**Get Help**).

2. Engine Cranks Slowly But Does Not Start

This is probably due to a low battery. Try a jump start (see page 101). If the engine then cranks normally and starts, your battery is low. Recharge it and see if the trouble occurs again. If it does happen again a short time later, you probably need a new battery. However, the trouble could be in the charging system. It is not keeping the battery charged (**Get Help**).

Note: If the engine cranks slowly in jump-starting it, there is probably trouble in the starting motor or in the engine. But consider this: "Is the battery in the *other* car up to charge?" Try the battery from still another car before you condemn the engine. During cold weather, engines are much harder to start and even a good battery may not be able to crank the engine very fast. (See page 86 on cold-weather starting.) *Also:* Perhaps the battery is run down from repeated tries at starting the engine. In this case, the trouble could be in the engine or the fuel or ignition system as noted in the following section.

3. Engine Cranks Normally But Does Not Start

The trouble could be in the fuel system, or in using the wrong starting procedure. Automotive diesel engines have glow plugs. These are little heaters located inside the engine cylinders (in the "precombustion" chambers). (See Figure 4-2.) In cold weather, when first starting, these plugs are connected to the battery. They warm up the precombustion chamber so there is enough heat to ignite the diesel fuel when it is injected (sprayed) into the engine precombustion chamber.

There are specific starting procedures that apply to automotive diesel engines. Refer to your owner's manual and

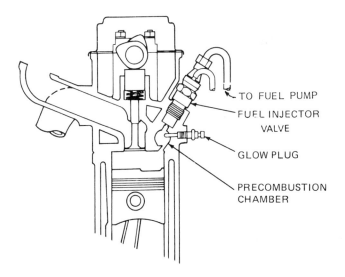

4-2 Automotive diesel engines have glow plugs which are located in the pre-combustion chambers. They pre-heat the air for easy starting of cold engines.

follow the procedure outlined there. For example, the starting procedure for one type of engine is:

    a. Put transmission lever in *park*.

    b. Turn the ignition switch to *run* (Fig. 4-3). Do not turn it to *start*. The amber *wait* light will come on

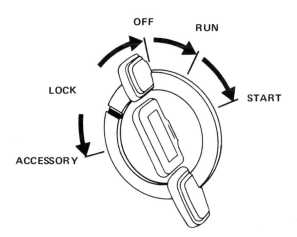

4-3 Ignition-switch positions for one automotive diesel engine. *(Oldsmobile Division of Geneal Motors Corporation)*

(Fig. 4-4). This means the glow plugs are on, heating the precombustion chambers.

c. After the chambers have been heated enough, the

GEN	OIL
HOT	BRAKE
WAIT	START

4-4 Instrument panel has two special lights, WAIT and START. The other four lights above them are warning lights for other components. *(Oldsmobile Division of General Motors Corporation)*

wait light will go out and the *start* light will come on. Now you turn the ignition switch to *start* to crank and start the engine. If the engine does not start in a few seconds, release the ignition switch. If the *wait* light comes on again, wait until it goes out and the *start* light comes on. Now try to start again. If the engine still will not start, there is probably trouble in the fuel system **(Get Help)**.

Note: It does no good to pump the gas pedal when trying to start. The diesel fuel system has no accelerator system, as in carburetors used in gasoline engines.

Fuel-system troubles the professional would look for would include incorrect or dirty fuel, fuel pump out of time, or defective or plugged fuel lines, and inoperative glow plugs.

Caution: Never use "starting aids" such as ether, gasoline, or similar materials in the diesel engine air intake. They can actually delay starting and can damage the engine.

ENGINE STARTS BUT STALLS ON IDLE

This is probably due to fuel-system problems. These include incorrect or dirty fuel, incorrectly-set idle speed, clogged injection valves, or an out-of-time or faulty pump. Internal engine problems might also be causing the trouble (**Get Help**).

ROUGH IDLE

This is probably due to fuel-system problems. These include incorrect or dirty fuel, incorrectly-set idle speed, clogged injection valves, or out-of-time or faulty pump (**Get Help**).

ENGINE LACKS POWER

Any condition in the fuel system that would prevent normal delivery of fuel to the engine cylinders would cause loss of engine power (**Get Help**). It could also be caused by a restricted exhaust (Fig. 2-7).

Did the loss of power happen all at once, just after you backed into a wall, or a high curb? You may have bent the exhaust pipe. This prevents normal engine exhaust and cuts down engine power. Or a collapsed inner layer of a laminated exhaust pipe (Fig 2-8) could be the cause. In either case (**Get Help**).

Other possible causes include:

1. *Transmission problems.* It may not be downshifting when you press the accelerator pedal to the floor. Also, the torque converter in the transmission may be bad (**Get Help**).

2. *Rolling resistance.* This may rob the engine of enough power so that you blame the engine. But the trouble could be due to low tires, dragging brakes, or wheel misalignment (**Get Help**).

3. *Internal engine troubles.* Defective or worn parts may cause engine problems (**Get Help**).

4. *Overheating engine.* See *Engine Overheats,* below.

ENGINE OVERHEATS

The temperature gauge or the red temperature light will warn you if the engine is overheating. If the gauge reads in the red danger area, or if the light comes on, pull off the road to a safe place and stop. If you continue to drive your risk radiator boilover (steam erupting from the radiator), and consequent serious damage to the engine. Open the hood to let engine heat escape.

Four things can cause engine overheating:

1. *A loose or broken fan belt* (pages 46 to 47).

2. *Loss of coolant* (water) from the engine cooling system (page 47).

3. *Driving* in slow-moving traffic on a hot day (page 19).

4. *Engine trouble.*

LOOSE FAN BELT

If the fan belt (Fig. 1-1) becomes worn or loose so that it slips and cannot drive the engine fan and water fast enough, the engine will overheat. You can check for a loose fan belt by turning the engine off and then pressing a thumb against the belt (Fig. 2-9). Be careful — if the belt has been slipping it will be hot!

Caution: The engine must be *off* when you test the belt. You could be seriously hurt if you touched the belt when the engine was running.

If you can push the belt in more than a half-inch, it is loose. It can be tightened by loosening the alternator brace and pulling out on the alternator while retightening the brace. Have the belt and tension checked at the next service station.

Note: A loose fan belt will sometimes make a squealing noise when you suddenly step on the gas. This happens when the engine picks up speed and there is a moment's lag during which the belt slips and squeals before it reaches engine speed.

BROKEN FAN BELT

If the fan belt (Fig. 1-1) breaks, you know it at once because the alternator stops charging. Without the belt, the engine fan and water pump stops and the engine will overheat in a few minutes. (See *Replacing a Broken Fan Belt* on pages 18 to 19 for what to do.)

Caution: Keep your hands and any dangling jewelry or loose clothing away from the fan belt and fan when the engine is running. The moving fan or fan belt can hurt you badly. Also, some transverally-mounted engines (engines mounted sideways) have electric-motor-driven fans (Fig. 2-11). The fan motor can turn on without warning with the engine warm and not running. Professionals disconnect the fan before working under the hood.

CHECKING COOLANT LEVEL

If the cooling system has an expansion tank (Fig. 2-10), you can readily see whether the coolant level is low. Otherwise, you will have to remove the radiator cap.

Caution: Never try to check the coolant level in the radiator if the engine is hot. The cooling system is pressurized. If you take the radiator cap off when the engine is hot, you release the pressure and a burst of steam and scalding water will erupt from the radiator. This could burn you seriously.

When the engine has cooled enough for you to hold your hand on the radiator cap, remove the cap and check the coolant level in the radiator. It should be up near the filler tube. If the coolant level is low, look for signs of leaks in your radiator or radiator hose. Antifreeze has dye in it to make leak detection easier. If you find a leak, you can usually make a temporary repair as explained on page 19, *Cooling System Temporary Repairs.*

If you see no signs of leaks, and the coolant level is more or less normal, perhaps the driving conditions have caused overheating. Driving in slow-moving traffic on a hot day can cause overheating. See *Hot-Weather Driving Hint* on page 19 for what to do.

ENGINE TROUBLES

If the overheating is not due to loss of coolant, a slipping or broken fan belt, or unusual driving conditions, you may have internal engine trouble. It could be that the engine has lost oil, or it has some internal damage (**Get Help**).

SMOKY EXHAUST

Technicians classify smoky exhaust as (1) *Blue Smoke,* (2) *Black Smoke,* or (3) *White Smoke.* This is what each means:

1. *Blue Smoke:* This probably means that worn engine parts are allowing lubricating oil to work its way into the engine cylinders, where it is burned. The remedy for this is an engine overhaul (**Get Help**).

2. *Black Smoke:* This is a signal that too much fuel oil is getting to the cylinders so that only part of it is burned. This leaves unburned or partly-burned fuel which is black and gives the exhaust a black color. The remedy is servicing the fuel system (**Get Help**).

3. *White Smoke:* This is steam. Coolant is leaking into the engine cylinders where it is turned into steam. Residue from the antifreeze can gum valves and piston rings and cause serious trouble. Replace gaskets and tighten cylinder-head bolts to eliminate the leakage (**Get Help**).

EXCESSIVE OIL CONSUMPTION

If you have to add crankcase oil to the engine frequently, the chances are you have an older, high-mileage engine. Cylinder walls and valve guides are probably worn, so excessive lubricating oil gets up into the combustion chambers where it is burned. The exhaust will be blue. The excessive oil consumption could be due to oil leaks from the engine (**Get Help**). Check the surface under your car where it is normally parked. If you find oil there, the engine is leaking oil (**Get Help**).

EXCESSIVE FUEL CONSUMPTION

This can result from many conditions, from the drivers style of driving to defects in the fuel system, engine, or drive train. A driver who floors the accelerator pedal when the light changes to green, and drives at high speeds, is going to burn extra fuel. The person who takes short trips around town is going to get poor fuel mileage.

Problems in the fuel system that feed too much fuel to the engine can cause poor fuel mileage. Any condition that causes poor engine performance, or engine missing, is going to increase fuel consumption. Fuel consumption will increase if the tires are low, if brakes drag, wheels are mis-aligned, or there are problems in the transmission and drive trains. As you can see, if the low fuel mileage is not the result of driving habits, professional help is needed to correct the problem.

ENGINE NOISES

The engine can make various noises, some that mean nothing, and others that signal something may be wrong. On pages 22 to 23 you will find a list of possible engine troubles and what could cause them. One noise that is unique to gasoline engines but not to diesel engines is pinging, discussed on page 22.

A noise that is unique to diesel engines is a "rapping" sound. This is due to air in the fuel line, or to an injection valve sticking partly open so it leaks fuel. If the noise is accompanied by black smoke exhaust, the injection-pump timing may be off, or the pump or engine has internal problems **(Get Help)**.

CHAPTER 5
Tire Troubles

Most tire troubles are caused by failure to keep the tires properly inflated, and by wheel misalignment. Before we discuss these further, we take a brief look at tire types and construction. Figure 5-1 shows the three basic types. The belted-radial tire is the most widely used today. Tire manu-

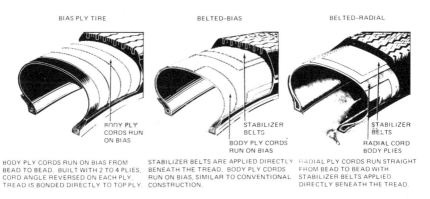

BIAS PLY TIRE

BELTED-BIAS

BELTED-RADIAL

BODY PLY CORDS RUN ON BIAS

STABILIZER BELTS

BODY PLY CORDS RUN ON BIAS

STABILIZER BELTS

RADIAL CORD BODY PLIES

BODY PLY CORDS RUN ON BIAS FROM BEAD TO BEAD. BUILT WITH 2 TO 4 PLIES. CORD ANGLE REVERSED ON EACH PLY. TREAD IS BONDED DIRECTLY TO TOP PLY.

STABILIZER BELTS ARE APPLIED DIRECTLY BENEATH THE TREAD. BODY PLY CORDS RUN ON BIAS, SIMILAR TO CONVENTIONAL CONSTRUCTION.

RADIAL PLY CORDS RUN STRAIGHT FROM BEAD TO BEAD WITH STABILIZER BELTS APPLIED DIRECTLY BENEATH THE TREAD.

5-1 The three basic tire constructions. *(Firestone Rubber Company)*

facturers say it lasts longer and it saves fuel because it offers less rolling resistance.

Car manufacturers strongly caution against mixing the different types of tires on a car. If you want belted-radial tires on your car, and it has bias-ply tires, you must buy five belted-radial tires. If you mix the tires on your car,

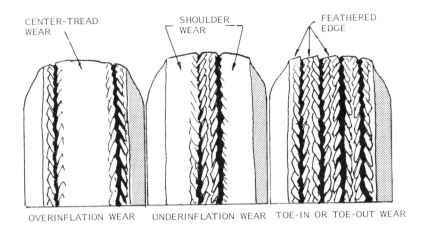

CENTER-TREAD WEAR

SHOULDER WEAR

FEATHERED EDGE

OVERINFLATION WEAR   UNDERINFLATION WEAR   TOE-IN OR TOE-OUT WEAR

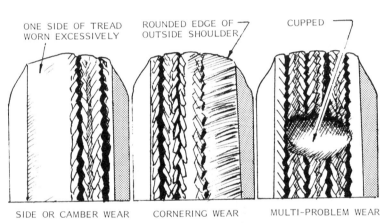

ONE SIDE OF TREAD WORN EXCESSIVELY

ROUNDED EDGE OF OUTSIDE SHOULDER

CUPPED

SIDE OR CAMBER WEAR   CORNERING WEAR   MULTI-PROBLEM WEAR

5-2   Patterns of abnormal tire wear. *(Buick Motor Division of General Motors Corporation)*

your car will be apt to spin or slide on wet or icy roads. The reason is that the tires have different rolling resistance and this can pull the car to one side and send it into a spin or slide.

TIRE WEAR

Figure 5-2 shows various kinds of abnormal tire wear. Here is what causes each:

1. *Shoulder Wear:* This is due to underinflation (Fig. 5-3). The tire is flattened enough so that the center of the tread is lifted clear of the road and only the two shoulders

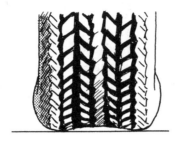

UNDER INFLATED

5-3   What happens with an underinflated tire. The main wear is on the tire shoulders.

take the wear. Keeping tires properly inflated will prevent this.

2. *Center-Tread Wear:* This is due to overinflation (Fig. 5-4). The tires will not give when rolling so that the

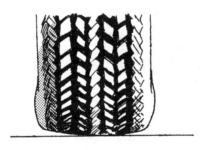

OVER INFLATED

5-4   What happens with an overinflated tire. The main wear is on the center of the tread.

wear is on the center part of the tread.

3. *Feathered Edge:* This kind of wear on tires on the front wheels is the result of incorrect front-wheel alignment **(Get Help)**.

4. *Side Wear:* This is due to misalignment of the wheels. The tires ride on only one side of the tread, and this side wears. The wheels should be aligned **(Get Help)**.

5. *Cornering Wear:* This is due to taking corners too fast so the tires skid sideways. The tread is worn off on the outside shoulder. The remedy is to slow down on turns.

6. *Uneven Wear:* The tread wear is spotty. It can be caused by misaligned wheels, unbalanced wheels, uneven or "grabby" braking, and out-of-round brake drums (**Get Help**).

TIRE CARE

Check tire pressure periodically and add air if necessary to bring the pressure up to the recommended level (page 83). Keep an eye on the tires so you will notice any abnormal wear as it begins to develop. You can then have the condition that is causing the abnormal wear corrected. This will increase tire life.

Many tires have wear indicators, which are filled-in sections of the tread grooves. When the tread has worn down enough to show the indicators (Fig. 5-5) it is time to get a

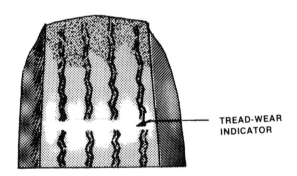

TREAD-WEAR INDICATOR

5-5 Tire treads have wear indicators. When the tread is worn down so much that the wear indicators show up, it is time to get a new tire. *(Chevrolet Motor Division of General Motors Corporation)*

new tire. A tire this worn has relatively little traction and more easily skids when going around a turn, or braking.

TIRE ROTATION

Tires can be switched from one position on the car to another in order to equalize wear. The right rear tire wears

BIAS-BELTED OR BIAS-PLY TIRES

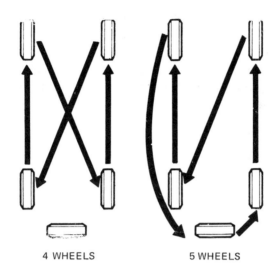

4 WHEELS   5 WHEELS

RADIAL TIRES

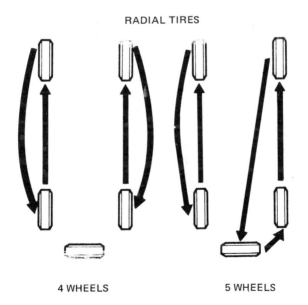

4 WHEELS   5 WHEELS

5-6   Tire-rotation diagrams for different types of tires.

about twice as fast as the left front tire, according to some studies that have been made. Figure 5-6 shows various tire-rotation diagrams for bias-belted or bias-ply tires, or for radial tires. Notice that radial tires are never switched from one side of the car to the other. This would reverse their direction of rotation and could result in handling and wear problems.

The mileage at which tires should be rotated will vary, according to the type of operation and wear the tires show. Rotate them when you notice significant differences in the tire wear.

TIRE REPAIR

Simple punctures can often be fixed without removing the tire from the rim. What the repair amounts to is inserting a rubber plug in the puncture hole (Fig. 5-7) and cut-

5-7 Tire cut away to show how the special needle pushes the plug into place through the puncture.

ting off the outer end (Fig. 5-8). The plug is applied with special vulcanizing fluid or rubber cement. Often, a satisfactory repair of small, simple puncture can be made on

5-8 After the needle is withdrawn, the plug is cut off at the tread level.

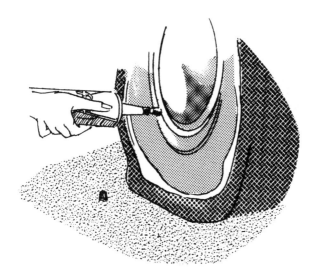

5-9 Small punctures may often be repaired on the road using the can of sealant-inflator in your emergency repair kit.

the road with a can of sealant-inflator (Fig. 5-9). Follow the instructions on the can.

For repair of bigger punctures, the tire should be removed from the rim and the puncture repaired from the inside of the tire **(Get Help)**.

CHANGING A TIRE

If you have a flat tire, don't try to stop quickly. Brake

lightly and slow gradually. Work your way well off the road to a level spot. Stop the engine and turn on the emergency flashers. Set the parking brake. Put the transmission in Park (automatic), or in Reverse (manual). Have everyone get out of the car on the side away from traffic. Now you are ready to change the tire.

Caution: Keep off the highway!

1. *Refer to your owner's manual* to find the correct points under which the jack is to be positioned.

2. *Open the trunk* and remove the tool kit and jack.

3. *Use a rock, or brick* or something similar to block the tire diagonally opposite the flat tire (Fig. 5-10). This will keep the car from rolling if it should slip off the jack.

4. *Pry off* the hub ornament or cover.

5. *Loosen all the wheel nuts* (Fig. 5-11) before jacking

5-10   Before jacking up the car to replace a flat tire, block the wheel diagonally opposite with stones or other objects.

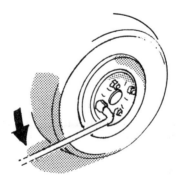

5-11   Loosen the wheel nuts before jacking up the car.

up the car.

6. *Position the jack* at the correct point and raise the car high enough so that the spare tire can be installed.

Caution: Never get under the car when it is supported only by a jack! The jack could slip and the car could fall on you.

7. *Remove the wheel nuts* and take off the wheel with the flat tire.

8. *Wipe the surface* on the brake drum or hub where the wheel is attached. This assures good contact on the mounting surface so the wheel nuts will not be apt to loosen.

9. *Roll the spare wheel and tire into position,* lift it up and align the holes with the bolts. Push the wheel into place and install the wheel nuts. Tighten them as much as you can with your fingers. Push the wheel tight onto the hub or drum and see if you can tighten the nuts any further with your fingers.

Note: If the spare is the collapsible type (Fig. 5-12), inflate it, using the can of propellant as explained on the can. This should be done before the car is lowered.

10. *Lower the car completely* and remove the jack.

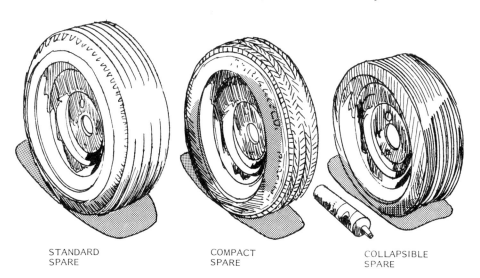

STANDARD
SPARE

COMPACT
SPARE

COLLAPSIBLE
SPARE

5-12   Three types of spare tires.

11. *Tighten, but do not overtighten the wheel nuts.* That is, do not use your foot on the wrench to get extra pressure. Tighten each nut just a little at a time, making the circuit several times. This draws the wheel evenly into place. At the service station where you will turn in your flat tire for repair, have the technician check the tightness of the wheel nuts with a torque wrench.

TYPES OF SPARE TIRES

There are three types of spare tires, the standard tire, the compact spare, and the collapsible spare (Fig. 5-12). We mentioned the collapsible type in the *Note,* above. After you install a compact or collapsible spare, you must observe the following precautions:

1. *Collapsible Spare:* Do not drive more than 150 miles (240 km) at a maximum speed of 50 miles per hour (80 km/h). To exceed these limits is to risk a blowout. Also, the collapsible spare must not be inflated from the usual air hose at the service station. This could cause the tire to explode. Reinstall the regular tire as soon as it is repaired. Collapse the spare before putting it back in the trunk.

2. *Compact Spare:* The compact spare is for emergency use only. As soon as you can get the flat tire repaired, reinstall it on the car. The compact spare carries an inflation pressure of up to 69 pounds per square inch (415 kPa). It will give you a rough and noisy ride.

CHAPTER 6
Brake Troubles

There are two types of automobile service brakes, drum brakes and disk brakes. Both operate in the same manner. Brake shoes or pads are forced with high pressure against a rotating drum or disk. Figure 6-1 shows the two types. The friction slows or stops the drum or disk and the wheel to which the drum or disk is attached. The pressure comes from the brake pedal being pushed down by the driver. This sends brake fluid at high pressure to the brake mechanisms at the wheels, causing the brakes to apply.

Cars also have parking brakes, which may use either drums or disks.

DUAL-BRAKING SYSTEM

The dual braking system consists of two separate braking systems, tied together only at the master cylinder under the brake pedal. One of these systems takes care of one pair of wheels. The other system takes care of the other pair of wheels. Figure 6-2 shows schematically the most common arrangement. The brake pedal, when pushed down, pushes the two pistons into the two sections of the master cylinder. This forces brake fluid from one section to the front-wheel cylinders. And it sends fluid from the other section to the rear-wheel cylinders.

The purpose of this dual braking system is to provide stopping power in case on section goes bad. The other section will still work and stop the car. But it will take longer

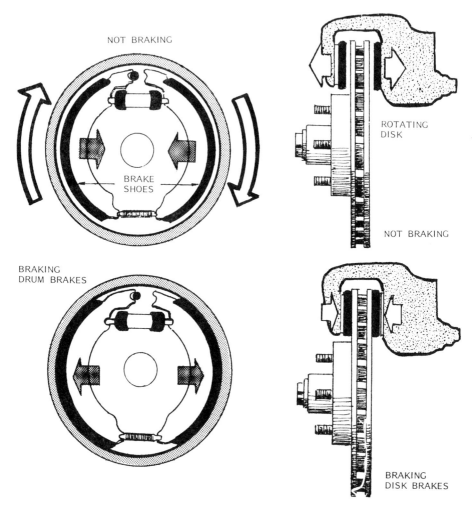

NOT BRAKING

ROTATING
DISK

BRAKE
SHOES

NOT BRAKING

BRAKING
DRUM BRAKES

BRAKING
DISK BRAKES

6-1　The two basic braking mechanisms at the wheels. The brake-drum has a pair of curved brake shoes that are pushed out for braking. The friction between the drum and brake shoe produces the braking action. The disk has flat pads, or shoes, on its two sides. The shoes are pushed in against the disk for braking.

and the brakes may have to be applied harder. Also, a brake warning light will come on. This light is on the instrument panel and warns the driver to get immediate service.

Caution: Never rely on only half the total braking system. Get service at once when the warning light comes

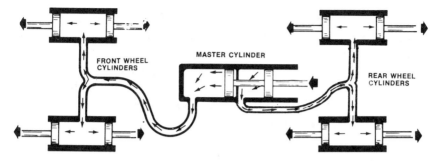

6-2 The dual braking arrangement has two separate brake systems, tied together only at the master cylinder.

on!

Many cars have power brakes, or brake boosters, as they are also called. They take over most of the braking effort, using engine vacuum to assist the brakes. If the engine should suddenly quit, you can still bring the car to a stop with normal braking pressure. The system has a reserve supply of vacuum to permit one or two stops.

If the engine stalls and you run out of vacuum, or if the brake booster quits, you can still stop the car. But it takes a much harder push on the brake pedal, and you won't stop as quickly. Get professional help at once.

DRUM BRAKE TROUBLES

Because drum brakes and disk brakes are constructed differently, they can have different kinds of trouble. We first look at drum brakes. Their troubles can include no braking, brake dragging, car pulls to one side when braking, soft or spongy brake pedal, and so on. In general, any brake problem requires professional help.

NO BRAKING

If the brake pedal goes to the floorboard without braking, the cause could be:
1. *Brake linkage or shoes out of adjustment.*
2. *Brake linings worn.*
3. Loss of brake fluid.

BRAKES DRAG

If any of the brake shoes drag on the brake drum, they will get very hot and lose brake effectiveness. Also, they can get so hot they will smoke. If this happens, get to the nearest service station without delay. Causes include:

1. *Resting a foot on the brake pedal.* This keeps the brakes partly applied so they drag and overheat.

2. *Incorrect linkage adjustment.*

3. *Clogged brake line.*

4. *Loose wheel bearing or bad wheel cylinder.*

5. *Bad master cylinder.*

6. *Mineral oil in system.* This can cause serious trouble. The oil causes the rubber piston rings and other parts to swell up so the brakes, once applied, will only partly release. Only the recommended brake fluid should be put into the brake system, *never* mineral oil.

CAR PULLS TO ONE SIDE WHEN BRAKING

This is due to uneven braking on the two sides of the car. The car pulls toward the side getting the better braking. Causes include:

1. *Brake linings soaked with oil or brake fluid* (this requires brake-lining replacement).

2. *Brake shoes out of adjustment.*

3. *Brake line clogged or a defective wheel cylinder.*

4. *Mismatched linings.* This could happen if you get a brake job and the new linings were installed uncorrectly.

5. *Uneven tire pressure.* Tire pressure should be as recommended in the owner's manual.

6. *Front end out of alignment* (see pages 103 to 105).

SOFT OR SPONGY PEDAL

If the brake pedal feels soft and spongy, chances are there is air in the system. Air can get in if brake fluid has leaked out so the master cylinder is low, or empty. When the brake pedal is pushed down, it compresses this air instead of forcing brake fluid to the brake cylinders. The air must be removed (by "bleeding" the system) after brake fluid is added. The leaks must be fixed **(Get Help)**.

EXCESSIVE PEDAL PRESSURE REQUIRED

This could be due to:

1. *Brake linings soaked with water.* This reduces brake action. You can dry the brakes by driving slowly with the brake pedal pushed down lightly. The action heats the linings so the water evaporates. Don't overdo!

2. *Brake linings hot or burned.* If you use the brakes excessively, as, for instance, when going down a long hill, you will overheat the linings and they will burn. When you are starting down a long hill, shift into a lower gear so the engine will help brake the car. You won't have to use the brakes so much. Burned linings must be replaced.

Note: Resting a foot on the brake pedal keeps the brakes partly applied so they drag and overheat.

3. *Power brake not working.* If his happens, you can still stop the car, but you will have to use a much harder push on the brake pedal. Get help at once.

BRAKES GRAB

If the brakes work unevenly, and suddenly grab when you press only lightly on the brake pedal, the cause could be:

1. *Brake linings soaked with oil or brake fluid.* The linings must be replaced.

2. *Power brake not working properly.* This must be serviced.

NOISY BRAKES

If the brake linings are worn, the rivets that attach the linings to the brake shoes may be rubbing on the brake drum, causing a squealing noise. The linings should be replaced at once. Continued operation may score the drums so they must be reground.

Other causes of noisy brakes include loose parts, warped shoes, or worn or rough brake drums.

WARNING LIGHT COMES ON WHEN BRAKING

This is a signal that one of the two sections of the dual braking system (see pages 61 to 63) has gone out. You have only half the normal braking action. Proceed slowly to the nearest service station to have the problem corrected.

DISK BRAKE TROUBLES

Disk-brake troubles include a different set of problems from drum brakes. This is because of the different construction of the mechanism at the car wheels (Fig. 6-1). Disk-brake troubles include excessive brake pedal travel, pedal pulsation, car pulling to one side, noisy brakes, and so on, as listed below.

EXCESSIVE BRAKE PEDAL TRAVEL
REQUIRED FOR BRAKING

This could be due to:

1. *Brake disk out of line.* This requires replacement of the disk.

2. *Air in system.* System must be "bled" while brake fluid is added. Then the system should be checked for leaks.

3. *Loose wheel bearing.* This must be readjusted.

4. *Power-brake working improperly.* It should be serviced.

BRAKE ROUGHNESS OR PEDAL PULSATION

If the pedal pulsates when you push it down, chances are the brake disk is out of line and wobbling. This causes the brake shoes to move in and out. The effect is felt back at the brake pedal. The brake disk must be replaced. Sometimes a loose wheel bearing causes the trouble. It should be adjusted.

CAR PULLS TO ONE SIDE WHEN BRAKING

This is due to uneven braking on the two sides of the car. The car pulls toward the side getting the better braking. Causes include:

1. *Brake fluid or oil on brake linings.* They must be replaced. Leaks must be repaired.

2. *Defects in wheel mechanisms* (calipers). They must be serviced.

3. *Unmatched linings.* This could happen if the wrong

linings were installed on only part of the calipers during a brake job.

4. *Uneven tire pressure.* Tire pressure should be as recommended in the owner's manual.

5. *Front end out of alignment* (see pages 103 and 104).

NOISY BRAKES

The brake shoes have tabs (called tell-tale tabs) that rub on the brake disk when the linings have worn down. This produces a high-pitched squeal that tells you it is time to have the linings replaced. Other noises could be due to loose brake parts or loose or worn wheel bearings.

BRAKES OVERHEAT

This could be due to excessive braking when going down a long hill. To avoid this, shift to a lower gear to let the engine do part of the braking. Other causes include the driver habitually resting a foot on the brake pedal; power-brake malfunction, or trouble, such as a sticking piston in a caliper (**Get Help**).

BRAKE PEDAL CAN BE PUSHED
DOWN WITHOUT BRAKING ACTION

This could be due to air in the system. The air must be bled as brake fluid is added and the system checked for possible leaks. Other causes could be a damaged master cylinder, or problems in the wheel calipers (**Get Help**).

WARNING LIGHT COMES ON WHEN BRAKING

This means that one of the two sections of the dual braking system (see pages 61 to 63) has gone out. You have only half the normal braking action. Proceed slowly to the nearest service station to have the problem corrected.

TIPS ON USING THE BRAKES PROPERLY

We have already mentioned that using the brakes excessively when going down a long hill can overheat them and burn the linings. Shift to a lower gear and let the engine do part of the braking.

Do not rest your foot on the brake pedal. This can cause the brakes to partly apply so they may overheat and burn. Also, this wastes fuel.

If the brake linings get wet, they are not as effective. We have mentioned what to do. Drive slowly with the brake pedal lightly held down. This heats up the linings and will quickly dry them. Don't overdo!

If you suddenly have a flat tire when driving, do not apply the brakes hard. Keep steering straight ahead and apply the brakes lightly to slow down. Sudden brake applications can cause the car to skid to one side. Pull off the road and stop. (See pages 57 to 60 on how to install the spare tire.)

When braking or stopping on wet or icy roads, easy does it! That is, do not apply the brakes hard or suddenly. If the car starts to skid, let up on the brakes so it straightens. Then apply the brakes again. Quick, light pats on the brake pedal will slow the car with less chance of sending the car into a spin.

Many cars with air conditioning have a fast idle that comes into action when the air conditioner is turned on. This prevents the added load of the air conditioner from stalling the engine. However, this can cause the car to creep forward when you stop with the air conditoner on. You may have to keep the brake applied to prevent this.

Always be sure the parking brake is released and the parking-brake light is off before shifting into gear and driving away.

CHAPTER 7
Steering and
Suspension Troubles

The suspension system includes springs that support the car body, and shock absorbers that control the spring action (Fig. 7-1). The suspension system is closely tied in with the steering system. When the driver turns the steering wheel, the front wheels swing to one side or the other (Fig. 7-2). That is, the driver points the front wheels in the direction the car should travel and the car follows. Figure 7-3 shows the connections between the steering wheel and the front wheels in a steering system using a steering gear. Figure 7-4 shows a rack-and-pinion steering system. Both are

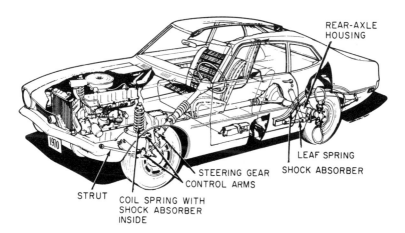

REAR-AXLE HOUSING

LEAF SPRING
SHOCK ABSORBER
STEERING GEAR
CONTROL ARMS
STRUT
COIL SPRING WITH SHOCK ABSORBER INSIDE

7-1 Cutaway car, showing details of the suspension system. *(Ford Motor Company)*

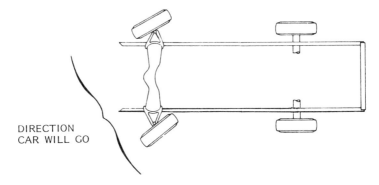

DIRECTION
CAR WILL GO

7-2 When the front wheels are turned to one side or the other, the car will follow in the direction the wheels are pointed.

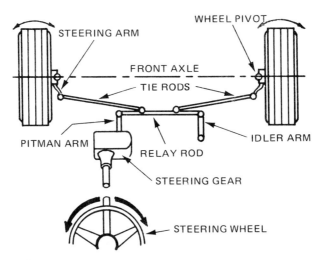

WHEEL PIVOT

STEERING ARM

FRONT AXLE

TIE RODS

PITMAN ARM

IDLER ARM

RELAY ROD

STEERING GEAR

STEERING WHEEL

7-3 Steering system. As the steering wheel is turned, the motion passes through the steering gear to the connecting linkage, causing the front wheels to turn to one side or other on their pivots.

simplified drawings which show only the essential details.

The front suspension system must allow the wheels to move up and down, and also allow them to swing from side to side so the driver can steer the car.

STEERING AND SUSPENSION TROUBLES

We look at both steering and suspension troubles to-

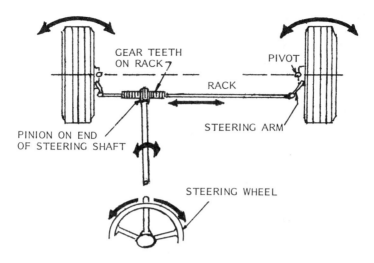

GEAR TEETH ON RACK

PIVOT

RACK

PINION ON END OF STEERING SHAFT

STEERING ARM

STEERING WHEEL

7-4 Rack-and-pinion steering system. As the steering wheel is turned, the pinion causes the rack to move to one side or the other. This causes the front wheels to swing on their pivots.

gether because the two systems are closely related, as noted above. Most steering and suspension troubles require professional help.

One thing you should ask yourself when you notice steering or suspension troubles is this: Did the trouble come on slowly? That is, did you have hints from time to time that something might be going wrong? Or did it come on suddenly, say, for example, after you accidentally hit that curb very hard when parking? These are things you would want to report to the technician when you have your car in for service.

Steering and suspension troubles can include:

EXCESSIVE PLAY IN THE STEERING SYSTEM

If you have to turn the steering wheel more than a few degrees before the front wheels respond, there is too much play — or looseness — in the steering system. This could be caused by looseness in the steering gear or linkage, or by worn supporting or connecting parts in the steering linkage. Also, loose wheel bearings can cause the trouble (**Get Help**).

HARD STEERING

If you have to exert excessive pressure to steer the car, the trouble could be:
1. *Power steering system not working.*
2. *Friction in the steering gear, linkage, or wheel supports.*
3. *Front alignment off* (see pages 103 to 105), *or frame bent.*
4. *Front spring sagging.*
5. *Low or uneven tire pressure.*

CAR WANDER

If you have to fight the steering wheel all the time to keep the car from wandering, the cause could be:
1. *Binding or too-loose steering linkage or steering gear.*
2. *Front alignment off* (see pages 103 to 105).
3. *Tire pressure low or uneven.*
4. *Unequal load in car.* (Heavy load on one side of the car.)

CAR PULLS TO ONE SIDE DURING DRIVING

If you have to apply continuous pressure on the steering wheel to keep the car going straight ahead, the trouble could be:
1. *Uneven tire pressure.* (Pressure is lower on one side.)
2. *Tight wheel bearing.*
3. *Front alignment off* (see pages 103 to 105).
4. *Uneven springs.* (One spring sagging, broken, or has loosened attachment.)
5. *Wheels not tracking.* (Rear wheels not following in line with the front wheels; this is due to bent frame.)

CAR PULLS TO ONE SIDE WHEN BRAKING

This is probably a braking problem. (See page 64 or 66-67.) It can also be caused by uneven tire pressure or front alignment being off (pages 103 to 105).

FRONT WHEEL SHIMMY AT LOW SPEEDS

Front-wheel shimmy and front-wheel tramp are sometimes confused. In front-wheel shimmy, the front wheels try to turn in and out, or oscillate, very rapidly. This causes the front end to shake from side to side. Front-wheel tramp, covered below, is the tendency for the front wheels to hop up and down.

Front-wheel shimmy can result from low or uneven tire pressure, loose linkage, soft springs, front end misalignment, or wheels out of balance (pages 103 to 104).

FRONT WHEEL TRAMP

Front-wheel tramp usually occurs at higher speeds. The wheels hop up and down and, in extreme conditions, will actually leave the pavement. The most common causes are unbalanced wheels, or wheels that are not in alignment. It can also be caused by front-end misalignment (pages 103 to 105). Defective shock absorbers which do not control spring action can also allow front-wheel tramp.

ROCKING MOTION

You feel this as continued bouncing of the front or rear end after you have passed a bump. That is, the car does not settle down after a bump. The reason is usually defective shock absorbers. They are not controlling the spring motion. You can check shock-absorber action on most cars as follows:

Lift up the bumper at one wheel, front or rear. Let it drop. The car should settle down to its normal height without bouncing. Step on the bumper to apply your weight and push it down. Step off to release the bumper. The car should rise to its normal height without bouncing. If the car continues to move up and down after you release it, the shock absorber at that wheel is defective. Repeat the test at the other three wheels.

STEERING KICKBACK

You experience this as sharp and rapid movements of the steering wheel that occur when the front wheels meet holes or bumps in the road. There will always be some

73

steering kickback, but when it becomes excessive, a professional should be consulted. Causes could be uneven or low tire pressure, sagging springs, defective shock absorbers, or looseness in the steering gear or steering linkage.

TIRES SQUEAL ON TURNS

This is due to taking curves at excessive speeds, low or uneven tire pressure, worn tires, or misaligned front end. Tires will wear more rapidly if you take curves too fast (see page 54).

IMPROPER TIRE WEAR

Pages 52 to 54 covers the various types of tire wear and what causes them.

HARD OR ROUGH RIDE

This can be caused by excessive tire pressure, defective shock absorbers, or excessive friction in the spring suspension.

SWAY ON TURNS

If the car sways, or leans outward excessively on turns, the cause could be defective shock absorbers, weak or sagging springs, misaligned front end (pages 103 to 105), or loose suspension parts.

NOISES

Noise could come from any loose, worn, or unlubricated part in the suspension or steering system.

CHAPTER 8
Drive Train Troubles

The drive train is the collection of subassemblies that carries the engine power to the car driving wheels. There

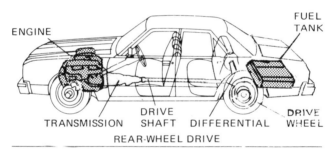

REAR-WHEEL DRIVE

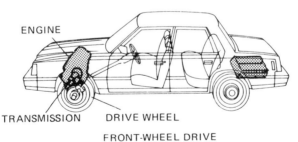

FRONT-WHEEL DRIVE

8-1   Two basic drive arrangements.

are three basic arrangements. Figure 8-1 shows the two most common types.

    1. *Engine at the front, rear wheels driven* (Fig. 8-2).

    2. *Engine at the front, front wheels driven* (Fig. 8-3).

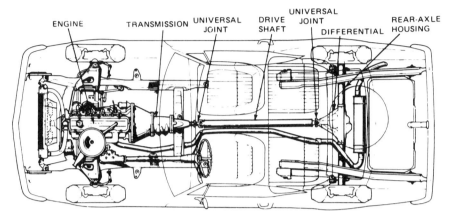

8-2   Details of a front-engine, rear-wheel drive arrangement. *(Chevrolet Motor Division of General Motors Corporation)*

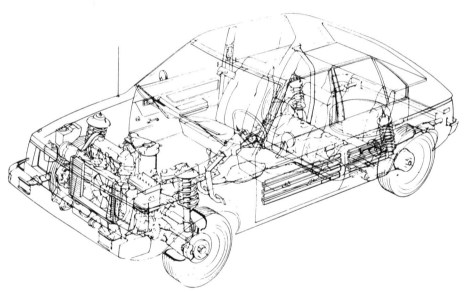

8-3   Details of a front-engine, front-wheel drive arrangement. *(Chrysler Corporation)*

3. *Engine at the rear, rear wheels driven.*

Another distinction to be made is whether or not the transmission is manually shifted, or is automatic. Automatic transmissions are in the great majority, but we will cover the manuals as well as the automatics.

ENGINE AT THE FRONT, MANUAL TRANSMISSION, REAR WHEELS DRIVEN

If this is the arrangement in your car, follow the list below to find the trouble you are having. Then note the possible causes under the heading. Chances are, whatever the cause is, you will need to take the car to a professional. But it will be good to know possible causes so you can talk to the professional intelligently. There are four basic components in this drive train, the clutch, the manual transmission, the drive shaft (or drive *line,* as it is also called), and the differential at the rear wheels.

TECHNICAL EXPLANATION

The clutch is a disconnecting mechanism. Its purpose is to momentarily disconnect the engine from the transmission so that gears in the transmission can be shifted. It is operated by a clutch pedal. When the pedal is pushed down, the engine is disconnected.

Note: A clutch is not used with automatic transmissions. Automatic transmissions have automatic clutches built into the transmission.

The transmission has a number of gears which allow the driver to change the rear ratio between the engine and the car wheels. When the transmission is in low gear, the engine can turn fast and put out considerable power. This power, applied to the stationary or slow-turning wheels, causes them to turn so the car moves. When the car speed has increased, the driver can shift gears to change the gear ratio. Now, the wheels turn faster and the car increases in speed without the engine turning at high speed. When the driver reaches a satisfactory speed, he or she shifts into a high gear. Now the car can cruise without the engine having to turn at high speed. When a car is cruising, the engine is producing only a part of the power it is capable of. However, with the engine "loafing along", as it were, fuel consumption is kept down.

The drive shaft is a long shaft that extends from the transmission at the front to the differential at the rear-wheel axles. The differential and rear wheels are moving up and down as the wheels meet bumps or holes in the road.

This causes the drive angle and the length of the drive shaft to change. To take care of these actions the drive shaft has joints (universal and slip).

The differential has several gears that can send different speeds to the rear wheels. When the car is going around a curve, the outside rear wheel must turn faster and travel farther than the inside rear wheel. The differential permits this to happen, continuing to send power to each rear wheel.

CLUTCH TROUBLES

As a rule any clutch trouble will require professional help. Causes include:

1. *Clutch slips while engaged.* This can be due to incorrect adjustment of the linkage between the clutch and the clutch pedal, a broken engine mount, or trouble inside the clutch.

Note: The engine is mounted on the frame at three or four places. If a mount breaks, the engine can move a little. This destroys engine-transmission-clutch alignment and may cause the clutch to slip.

2. *Clutch chatters or grabs when engaged.* This can be due to binding in the clutch linkage, a broken engine mount, or internal damage.

3. *Clutch spins or drags when disengaged.* This can result from incorrect clutch-linkage adjustment, a broken engine mount, or internal damage.

4. *Clutch noises — clutch engaged.* This is probably due to loose or damaged parts in the clutch, or to misalignment of the engine and transmission.

5. *Clutch noises — clutch disengaged.* This is probably due to wear, or lack of lubricant, or to internal clutch problems.

6. *Clutch pedal pulsations.* If you feel a pulsation as you push the clutch pedal down, the trouble is probably due to the engine and transmission being out of line.

7. *Stiff clutch pedal.* This is due to lack of lubricant in the clutch linkage, or to the overcenter spring being misadjusted.

MANUAL TRANSMISSION TROUBLES

Most manual transmission troubles are due to the gear-shift linkage being out of adjustment or needed lubrication, or to wear or damage inside the transmission. In any case, you will need professional help. Here are possible troubles and causes:

1. *Hard shift into gear.* The linkage is out of adjustment or needs lubricating, or there is trouble in the transmission (gears binding on shafts, gears damaged, synchronizer damaged, etc.)

2. *Transmission sticks in gear.* The gearshift linkage is out of adjustment or needs lubricating, or there is trouble in the transmission.

3. *Transmission slips out of gear.* The gearshift linkage is out of adjustment or there is trouble inside the transmission.

4. *No power through the transmission.* The clutch is slipping or there is serious damage inside the transmission.

5. *Transmission noisy.* There is internal trouble; gears are damaged or, the bearings are worn or dry. Also, the noise may be coming from the clutch.

6. *Gears clash in shifting.* Sometimes, if you attempt to shift too fast, you can cause gear clash. If gears clash when you try to shift normally, the trouble is due to internal transmission trouble, or to failure of the clutch to fully release.

DRIVE-LINE (SHAFT) TROUBLES

The drive line carries engine power from the transmission to the differential at the rear wheels (Fig. 8-2). It has joints that permit the shaft to lengthen or shorten, and to change angles, as the rear wheels and differential move up and down. In many cars these joints are permanently lubricated and should never give trouble. If the car is in an accident, or the transmission or differential is removed for service, driveshaft balance and alignment may be lost. This could cause the driveshaft to vibrate and produce a noticeable shaking at certain speeds. The driveshaft must be realigned and balanced (**Get Help**).

DIFFERENTIAL TROUBLES

Most often, it is noise that calls attention to differential trouble. The noise may be a hum, growl, or knock. Sometimes tire noise is mistakenly blamed on the differential. To eliminate this possibility drive on different types of roads. If the noise is about the same regardless of the type of pavement, then the trouble is probably inside the differential. You should get professional help as soon as you notice the noise. It could be due to worn bearings or gears and could get worse to the point where serious damage will result. However, if the differential is serviced before serious damage takes place, it could require only an adjustment and not replacement of parts or of the differential itself.

ENGINE AT THE FRONT, AUTOMATIC TRANSMISSION, REAR WHEELS DRIVEN

This arrangement (Fig. 8-1) is similar to the front-engine, rear-wheel-drive using a manual transmission. The basic difference is that the automatic transmission needs no clutch, and it automatically selects the proper gear for the driving condition.

The drive-line and differential problems discussed for the arrangement using the manual transmission are the same for the automatic-transmission arrangement.

Problems with the automatic transmission all require professional help. The transmission has internal clutches, planetary gears, a torque converter (a sort of fluid clutch), and other parts that work hydraulically (from pressure on transmission oil). It takes a trained technician, with the proper tools and testers, to properly service automatics, and correct problems.

Troubles that might occur include wrong or erratic upshifts or downshifts, rough shifts, failure to shift properly, and noises. Some of these troubles can be solved by an adjustment. Others may require disassembly of the transmission to replace worn or defective parts.

ENGINE AT THE FRONT, FRONT WHEELS DRIVEN

This arrangement (Fig. 8-3) is used on many of the

newer small, fuel-efficient cars. The engine is mounted sideways (transversally) and the transmission (manual or automatic) and differential are attached to the engine. The clutch (on manual transmissions), transmission, and differential are combined into a single unit, called the *transaxle*. The transaxle is mounted on the engine. This arrangement is space-saving and simplifies the mounting of the components.

The clutch (for manual transmissions), the transmission, either manual or automatic, and the differential are very similar to the separate units used in front engine, rear-wheel driven cars. The troubles they might have are also similar. Refer to page 78. Note that any troubles in the transaxle will probably require the services of a professional to correct.

ENGINE AT THE REAR, REAR WHEELS DRIVEN

This arrangement has been on some cars, the Volkswagen Beetle, for example. The clutch (where used), the transmission, and the differential are all mounted together to the engine. These components are very similar to those used in the engine at the front, rear wheels driven arrangement. Troubles with the units are also similar. Refer to pages 78 to 79. Note that any troubles with these components will probably require the services of a professional to correct.

CHAPTER 9
Driving Hints

Here are some driving hints that can save you money by saving fuel and making your car last longer.

1. *Check tire pressure regularly* and correct it if the pressure is low. The best time is in the morning, before starting out. Once on the road, the tires get hot and internal pressure goes up. If the pressure is checked with the tire hot, it may read high. If it does, do not bleed air to reduce pressure. Wait and check again when the tire has cooled off.

Remember: Low tire pressure increases fuel consumption and wears the tire shoulders (Fig. 5-3). High pressure wears the center of the tread (Fig. 5-4).

Note: Keep an eye on your tires to check for abnormal wear (see pages 52 to 54). If you notice abnormal wear, get professional help to correct the trouble causing it. If you do not do this, tire life will be shortened.

2. *Avoid "jack-rabbit" starts, and erratic driving* (speeding up, braking, speeding up again). These driving habits waste fuel and increase wear on the brakes. Try to maintain a steady pace and anticipate the traffic conditions and traffic signals. Instead of dashing up to the stop sign, slamming on the brakes, and then speeding away when the light changes, try coasting so the car slows down more gradually. Then move off smoothly when you get the "go" sign.

3. *Idle for a short time,* when first starting out (espe-

cially in cold weather), and then take off. This gets the oil circulating and starts engine warmup. But do not idle too long — this wastes fuel.

4. *Never rest your foot on the brake or clutch pedal.* This can overheat and wear the clutch or brakes and wastes fuel.

5. *Keep the front wheels in proper alignment.* If the front end is out of alignment, tires will wear faster (pages 103 to 105) and your car will use more fuel. Avoid hitting the curb and potholes or bumps in the road as much as possible. If you notice that the car seems to pull to one side, especially after you have accidentally hit a curb hard, get the alignment checked. Also, keep an eye on the front tires. If you notice unusual wear (pages 52 to 54), get the front alignment checked and corrected.

6. *Keep the car tuned up* and follow the maintenance schedule as described in your owner's manual. See pages 102 to 103.

7. *Watch the gauges and trouble lights,* as noted below.

WATCHING THE GAUGES AND TROUBLE LIGHTS

All cars have indicators — gauges, or lights — on the instrument panel. These warn you if something is going wrong. The three most important are the fuel gauge, the engine temperature light or gauge, and the engine oil light or gauge. Here is how they warn you and what you should do when you are warned:

1. Fuel Gauge

This is the gauge you usually watch. It's no fun to run out of fuel. So when the gauge shows low, pull into a service station promptly to get your tank filled up. Some of the newer cars have an electronic gadget that shows how many more miles you can go before the fuel runs out. Some of these cars have a speaking computer that tells you when the fuel is running low.

2. Temperature Light or Gauge

If the temperature gauge needle moves over into the red danger area, of if the red temperature light comes on, the engine temperature has risen to the danger point. Pull over to a safe place to stop. Open the hood to let engine heat escape. If you continue to drive you could ruin the engine.

The trouble could be due to loss of coolant through leaks, or to a broken fan belt (page 16). See also *Hot Weather Driving Hint* (page 19) for a hint on how to prevent engine overheating in hot weather when stuck in slow-moving traffic.

3. Engine Oil Light or Gauge

If the oil gauge reads low, or the oil light suddenly comes on, or flickers on and off, the engine is in serious danger. The engine is not getting enough lubricating oil. Pull over at once in a safe place and shut off the engine. Running an engine without enough lubricating oil can quickly ruin it.

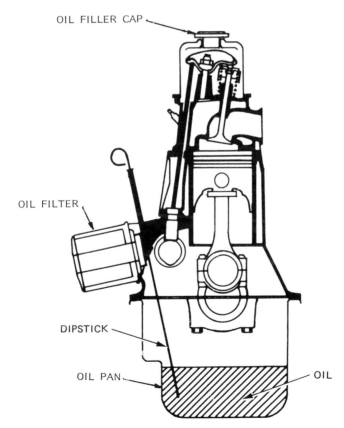

OIL FILLER CAP

OIL FILTER

DIPSTICK

OIL PAN

OIL

9-1 Dipstick location.

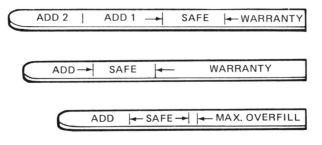

9-2   Markings on various dipsticks.

Check the dipstick (see Figs. 1-1, 9-1 and 9-2). To do this, first pull out the dipstick and wipe it off. Then reinsert it and pull it out again. If the level is well below the *"Add"* mark, or if the dipstick shows no trace of oil, add oil. You should carry at least one quart of oil in your trunk. It is part of your emergency repair kit (Fig. 1-2). Stop at the next service station to have the oil checked again. You may need to add more oil. When putting the dipstick back, be sure to insert it all the way.

COLD WEATHER STARTING AND OPERATION

Starting and operating a car in cold weather is more difficult. However, there are certain things you can do to make it easier.

1. *Make sure your antifreeze protection is adequate* for the lowest temperature the car may encounter. Antifreeze strengh is checked with a special hydometer. If it is not adequate, add more antifreeze.

2. *Make sure the battery is in good condition and charged.* Check the electrolyte level if the battery has caps (and is not a maintenance-free battery). If the level is low, add water. Check the condition of the battery cables and connections (pages 98 to 100) and make corrections as needed.

3. *Make sure that the windshield-washer fluid has antifreeze in it.* This is a special antifreeze that will not damage the car paint. Never use cooling-system antifreeze — it can spot the paint.

4. *Make sure your car is tuned-up* before cold

weather really sets in. Then the ignition system, the fuel system, the starting system, and engine, will be ready for the cold weather.

5. *Make periodic checks of your car* when driving through snow and slush. Stop occasionally to see if ice is accumulating under the fenders. Ice can make steering and car control difficult. Break the ice loose, being careful to avoid damaging the fenders.

6. *Make your car door locks freeze-resistant.* If you have trouble with a door lock freezing, squirt some de-icer into it. One way to unfreeze a lock is to heat the key with a match before inserting it. This usually melts the ice in the lock enough to enable you to unlock the door.

7. *Make sure you can safely park.* If conditions are bad — slush, freezing rain — there may be some danger of the parking brake freezing up if you apply it when you stop. Instead, put the transmission in "P" (automatic) or in first, or reverse (manual). If on a hill, park next to the curb and turn the front wheels in or out as an added safeguard against the car moving.

8. *Make sure the engine oil has the proper viscosity* for cold-weather operation. Also, be sure the fuel you are using is suited to cold weather.

9. *Make sure you have your emergency kit* (Fig. 1-2).

10. *Make sure you know about cold weather starting.* If the battery is up-to-charge, and you follow the recommended starting procedure, you should have no special starting problems. See your owner's manual.

In extremely cold weather, some drivers use block heaters. These are electric heaters installed in the engine or engine compartment. They have a plug-in so they can be connected to the 110-volt house current. A small electric heater placed in front of the car radiator is also a big help.

EMERGENCY REPAIR KIT

Figure 1-2 shows the complete package and everything required for a complete emergency kit. You may drive for years and never need anything from the kit. But if you do have an emergency, it is comforting to know that you can reach into the trunk and come up with the very item you need to get you going again.

CHAPTER 10
Maintenance and Service

There are certain things you should check daily, or whenever you use your car. There are other checks to be made whenever you get fuel. There are also services that the car requires at periodic intervals (mileage or months of operation).

DAILY CHECKS

1. *Look at the tires* to see if they appear to be properly inflated. If they look low, check the pressure and add air if necessary.

2. *Look at the fuel gauge* after starting. Then notice whether the alternator is charging the battery. Also, see that the oil gauge shows normal pressure (or the oil warning light is off). After driving a while, keep an eye on the engine temperature gauge (or the temperature warning light) to see if the engine is overheating (page 15).

3. *Listen for any unusual noises* as you drive. Also, ask yourself: Is the engine performing okay? Steering okay?

Suspension acting normally? By being alert to detect anything unusual, you may be able to spot a trouble that is beginning to develop. You can get it fixed before it develops into something serious.

FUEL STOP CHECKS

When you stop for fuel, you can have the level of the engine oil in the crankcase checked (pages 85 to 86). Notice the condition of the fan belts and if they are adjusted tightly enough. (*Engine off!*) Look at the battery to see if it appears normal (pages 98-100). Also, check the level of the windshield-washer fluid. In addition, if your cooling system has an expansion tank, you can check the level of the coolant. Periodically you should have the tire pressures checked and air added if necessary.

You may not want to have all of these services performed every time you stop for fuel. But be sure to have them done often enough to keep you aware of what is going on under the hood.

PERIODIC MAINTENANCE SCHEDULE

A number of services and checks should be performed at periodic intervals: number of miles, or kilometers, or number of months. The chart that follows has been adapted from maintenance schedules for late-model cars. The owner's manual for your car has a similar maintenance schedule. All such schedules are pretty much alike. The schedule tells you what components of the car should be checked or serviced and at what recommended intervals (distance driven, or number of months the car has been in use). For example, the schedule calls for changing the engine oil every 7,500 miles (12,000 km) or 12 months, whichever comes first. If the car is used in severe service, the oil should be changed more often. See the *Note* on page 92.

Explanations of the various services follow the chart.

MAINTENANCE SCHEDULE FOR CARS WITH GASOLINE ENGINES

(Typical only. See owner's manual for your car.)

When to Service: Miles (Mi), Kilometers (Km), or Months (Mo).

+: Inspect at 15,000 Mi (24,000 Km).
- A: Replace at 30,000 Mi (48,000 Km).
- B: Drain, flush, refill at 30,000 Mi (48,000 Km).

What to Service	12 Mo 7,500 Mi 12,000 Km	24 Mo 15,000 Mi 24,000 Km	36 Mo 22,500 Mi 36,000 Km	48 Mo 30,000 Mi 48,000 Km	60 Mo 37,500 Mi 60,000 Km	72 Mo 45,000 Mi 72,000 Km
1. Chassis lubrication	•	•	•	•	•	•
2. Engine oil change	•	•	•	•	•	•
3. Oil filter change	•		•		•	
4. Tire checks	•	•	•	•	•	•
5. Checking fluid levels	•	•	•	•	•	•
6. Spark plugs				•		
7. Air cleaner		+		• A		
8. Cooling system		+		• B		
9. Battery	•	•	•	•	•	•
10. Tune-up				•		
11. Front-end alignment and wheel balance	As Necessary					

1. CHASSIS LUBRICATION

The various chassis components that should be lubricated periodically include the front suspension, steering and transmission-shift linkage, hood latches, door-lock cylinders, fuel-tank-filler door hinge, door hinges, parking brake linkage, and gas-pedal linkage. Special lubricants are required for these (**Get Help**).

2. ENGINE OIL CHANGE

The engine oil should be changed every 7,500 miles

(12,000 km) or 12 months, whichever comes first. The first time the oil is changed on a new car, the oil filter should also be changed. After that the oil filter should be changed every second oil change.

Note: If the car is in severe service, the oil and oil filter should be changed more often — every 3,000 miles (4,800 km) or 3 months, whichever comes first. Severe service is defined as operating in dusty areas, idling for extended periods, low-speed operation, towing a trailer, operating in continuing below-freezing weather, and using the car for short trips only (four miles or 6 km or less). Severe service vehicles would include taxis, door-to-door delivery, trucks and police cars.

To change oil, have on hand the correct amount of the engine oil recommended for your car. Also, have the proper oil filter if you are also going to change it.

With the engine warm, so the oil will flow freely, put a pan large enough to hold the engine oil under the oil-drain hole in the oil pan. Loosen the drain plug with a wrench and then remove it by hand (Fig 10-1). Let the oil drain into the pan (Fig. 10-2).

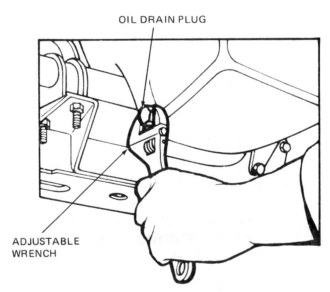

OIL DRAIN PLUG

ADJUSTABLE
WRENCH

10-1   Removing drain plug from the oil pan. *(Chrysler Corporation)*

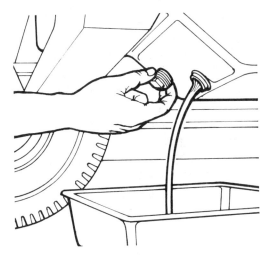

10-2   Draining the oil from the engine. *(Chrysler Corporation)*

Caution: If the oil is hot, it can burn you. Hold your arm up when removing the plug so the oil does not run down to your elbow.

After the oil has drained, replace the drain plug and tighten it to the proper tension. Do not overtighten it! Be sure the drain-plug gasket is in good condition.

Remove the oil filler cap (Fig. 9-1). Add the proper amount of the correct oil to the crankcase. Replace the oil filler cap. Start the engine. Watch the oil indicator light or gauge. The light should glow or the gauge read low for only a few seconds. Then the light should go out or the gauge should come up to normal pressure.

Run the engine for about five minutes. Shut it off and check around the drain plug (and oil filter if you have changed that) for leaks. Then check the crankcase oil level with the dipstick to make sure the crankcase is filled to the proper level. Use a lubrication sticker, or write on the sticker that is in place, the date and mileage when the oil was changed.

3. OIL FILTER CHANGE

As mentioned above, the first time the oil is changed on

a new car, the oil filter should be changed. After that the oil filter should be changed every other oil change.

To change the filter, first drain the crankcase oil. Install the drain plug. Do not add fresh oil until after the filter is changed. Put the drain pan under the filter to catch the oil that will drain out. Loosen the oil filter a couple of turns. Allow the oil in it to drain out. Then remove the filter. Put it in the drain pan, gasket end up.

Make sure the old filter gasket is not on the engine. Clean the engine surface where the new filter gasket will fit. Check the old and new filters to make sure they are the same size and type. If the new filter is larger, make sure it will fit without interference with the frame and suspension.

Coat the face of the gasket on the new filter with clean oil. If the filter will be in an upright position when mounted on the engine, fill it with engine oil. Then carefully thread the filter into the engine mounting hole. Hand-tighten it until the gasket makes contact with the engine gasket surface. Now tighten the filter another half turn to make sure it is securely tightened. Wipe the filter and mounting surface clean.

Fill the crankcase with oil as noted above under *Engine Oil Change.* Start the engine and watch the oil-pressure gauge or light. If normal pressure shows after a few seconds, all is well. Check around the oil drain plug and oil filter to make sure there are no leaks.

Recheck the oil level with the dipstick and add oil to the crankcase if necessary. Use a lubrication sticker, or write on the sticker that is in place, the date and mileage when the filter was changed.

4. TIRE CHECK

Abnormal tire wear and its causes are described on pages 52 to 54. Tires should be kept properly inflated (page 83). At periodic intervals they should be rotated (changed from one position on the car to another, as explained on pages 54 to 56).

5. CHECKING FLUID LEVELS

Several fluids are used in the car. We have already described checking and changing engine lubricating oil (pages

91 to 93). We have also described checking the coolant level in the cooling system (pages 16 to 17). Other fluids include brake fluid, power-steering-pump fluid, transmission fluid, and lubricant in the differential.

The levels of these fluids should be checked periodically. This is usually done during chassis lubrication or during a tune-up (pages 102 to 103).

Note: Low brake fluid in the master cylinder of a disk-brake system could mean worn brake linings in the brake pads. It could also mean a leak in a brake-line connection or a wheel mechanism.

6. REPLACING SPARK PLUGS

Spark plugs should be replaced periodically. The chart recommends replacement every 30,000 miles (48,000 km). There is no special problem in replacing spark plugs. Here is a typical procedure.

You will probably need a long socket to reach down into the spark-plug well to loosen the plug. Do not pull on the spark-plug cable to disconnect it from the plug. This can damage the cable. Instead, grasp the rubber boot and twist and pull on it (Fig. 2-3).

Before the plugs are unscrewed, any accumulation of dirt around the spark plugs must be removed so it won't fall into the engine. One way of removing the dirt is to blow it away with compressed air. Another way is to loosen the plugs a little and then start the engine. The leakage of compression around the plugs will blow away any dirt.

Some plugs are mounted in deep wells. To reach these, you need a special spark-plug socket which has a rubber boot. This boot grips the spark-plug insulator so the plug can be pulled out after it is unscrewed.

If the new plugs use gaskets, be sure they are in place when installing the plugs. Also, make sure the old gaskets have been removed from the engine. Tighten the plugs properly. A torque wrench is recommended.

When reconnecting the spark plug cables, push them on the plugs by pushing through the boots. Squeeze the boots to eliminate any air trapped under the boots.

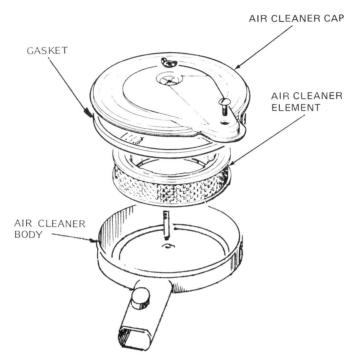

AIR CLEANER CAP

GASKET

AIR CLEANER
ELEMENT

AIR CLEANER
BODY

10-3 Location of the air-cleaner element under the cap.
(American Motors Corporation)

7. AIR CLEANER

The air cleaner element should be replaced periodically as noted in the maintenance schedule. There is nothing special about replacing the cleaner element. You take off the air-cleaner cap and remove the cleaner element (Fig. 10-3). Before installing the new element, clean the bottom of the air cleaner and the gasket surfaces. The cover seal should be in good condition so it seals tightly. Even a pinhole opening might let in enough dust to damage the engine after a few thousand miles.

When installing the element and the air-cleaner cap, be sure that the gasket surfaces seal tightly, top and bottom. The air cleaner has hoses attached. Be sure they are not loosened when you are installing the new element.

8. COOLING SYSTEM

The cooling system should be checked frequently. All

this normally means is to look at the expansion tank to make sure the coolant level is up to normal. If the level is low, add water and antifreeze. Check for leaks (pages 16 to 17 and 19).

The cooling system should be drained, flushed out, and refilled with coolant every 24 months or 30,000 miles (48,000 km). This procedure is usually done at a service station. However, you can do it yourself. Let the engine cool. Then drain the cooling system by removing the radiator cap and opening the engine and radiator drain cocks (Fig. 10-4). Use the garden hose to run water through the radiator and engine. Continue until the water from the drain cocks runs clear.

Then close the two drain cocks. Fill the system with a mixture of water and antifreeze. Read the instructions on the antifreeze can to determine the proportions of water and antifreeze in the mixture. One recommended way is to

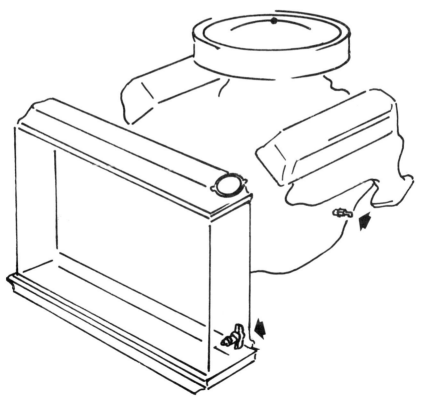

10-4   Locations of cooling system drain cocks on the radiator and engine. Locations are different on different cars.

pour the right amount of antifreeze in first, and then fill the radiator with clean water. Fill the expansion tank to the *Full* level. Start the engine. As it warms up, the coolant in the radiator may drop. Add water to bring it up to the fill level again.

Install the radiator and expansion-tank caps. Recheck the drain cocks to make sure they are not leaking.

Note: At the time that you drain, flush, and refill the radiator, check the radiator hoses to make sure they are in good condition and that the connections are tight

Caution: Keep hands, jewelry, and loose clothing away from the fan and fan belt when the engine is running. You could be seriously hurt if you tangled with the fan or belt. Also, some transversally-mounted engines (engines mounted sideways) have electric-motor-driven fans (Fig. 2-11). The motor can turn on without warning with the engine warm and not running. Professionals disconnect the fan before working under the hood.

9. BATTERY

Many batteries are the "no-maintenance" type. They have no vent caps. The only maintenance they require is to make sure the hold-clamps and cable connections are tight. Many of these have a charge indicator in the battery top.

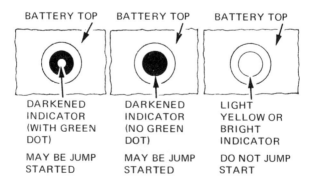

BATTERY TOP	BATTERY TOP	BATTERY TOP
DARKENED INDICATOR (WITH GREEN DOT)	DARKENED INDICATOR (NO GREEN DOT)	LIGHT YELLOW OR BRIGHT INDICATOR
MAY BE JUMP STARTED	MAY BE JUMP STARTED	DO NOT JUMP START

10-5 Different colors of the battery charge indicator and what they mean. *(Delco-Remy Division of General Motors Corporation)*

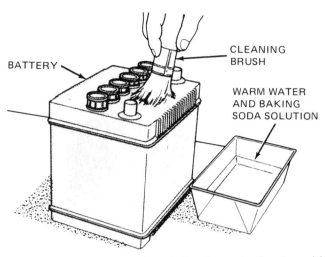

BATTERY

CLEANING BRUSH

WARM WATER AND BAKING SODA SOLUTION

10-6   Brushing on baking-soda solution to neutralize the acid and clean the battery top.

Its appearance will tell you whether or not the battery is up to charge (Fig. 10-5).

Other batteries have vent caps (Fig. 10-6) which can be removed to check the electrolyte level. If it is low, add distilled water. Do not overfill! Some batteries have transparent cases so you can see whether or not water is needed without removing the vent caps.

Caution: Batteries contain sulfuric acid. This acid is very corrosive and can give you severe burns. If it gets on your skin, wash it off with plenty of water. If the area feels burned, get to a doctor at once! If you get battery liquid in your eyes, flush your eyes with clean water (Fig. 10-7) for at least 15 minutes. Then get to a doctor at once! Continue to apply water to the eyes with a cloth or sponge on the way to the doctor's office. Wear safety goggles when working around batteries, to protect your eyes.

If electrolyte gets on your clothes, take them off at once. It can soak through to the skin and burn you severely. The clothes will probably be ruined because the acid will eat the cloth.

Caution: Batteries give off explosive hydrogen gas.

10-7   Flushing the eye to remove acid that has been splashed into it. Continue to flush for 15 minutes and get to a doctor at once.

Never cause sparks from the battery when working around it with tools. Do not smoke or have a flame around batteries. They could explode. When charging a battery, have adequate ventilation to prevent the accumulation of explosive hydrogen gas.

If the top of the battery is dirty, and the cable clamps corroded, disconnect the cable clamps. Disconnect the grounded cable clamp first. This is the cable that is connected to the engine or car frame. Then disconnect the insulated cable clamp. This avoids accidental grounding of the insulated side of the system with a resulting heavy sparking and possible damage to the electrical system. Scrape off the corrosion from the battery terminal posts and the cable clamps with a knife. Make sure the vent plugs are tight. Then brush on a solution of water and baking soda (Fig. 10-6). This will neutralize any acid on the battery top. Flush off the solution with clean water. Refasten the cable clamps. Put a dab of grease on top of the cable clamps and terminal posts to retard corrosion.

JUMP-STARTING YOUR CAR

If your battery is run down so you cannot start, you can connect the battery from another car to help you get started. The procedure is called jump-starting. Here is how it is done.

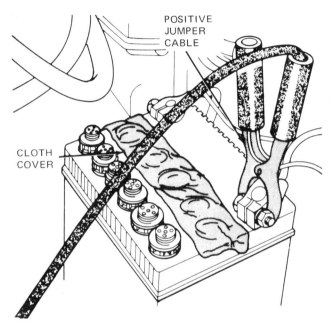

POSITIVE
JUMPER
CABLE

CLOTH
COVER

10-8   Covering vent-cap openings with cloth, and connecting the jumper cable to one terminal.

1. Wear eye protection. Do not lean over the batteries.

2. Loosen or remove the vent plugs and cover the holes with cloths (Fig. 10-8).

3. If the battery is the maintenance-free type, and the charge indicator shows yellow, do not try to jump-start. The battery is defective. Connecting a good battery could cause the defective battery to explode!

4. If the dead battery has frozen, connecting a good battery to it could cause it to explode.

5. Use a jump battery of the same voltage as the battery in your car. Some cars have a six-volt batteries. Most have 12-volt batteries. Some have 24-volt batteries. If you

101

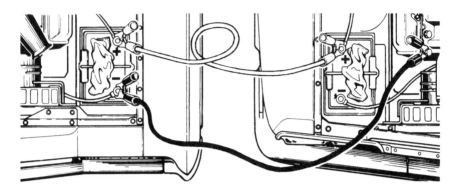

10-9   Connections between a booster battery and the dead battery to jump-start the car with a dead battery.

use a battery of the wrong voltage, one or both batteries may explode and you could ruin the electrical equipment on one or both cars.

Here is the jump-start procedure. See Figure 10-9.

1. With the vent plugs removed and the holes covered with cloth, connect the end of one jumper cable to the positive (+) terminal of the good battery. Connect the other end of this cable to the positive (+) terminal of the dead battery.

2. Connect one end of the second cable to the negative (−) terminal of the good battery.

3. Connect the other end of the second cable to the engine block of the car you are trying to start. Do not connect it to the negative terminal of the dead battery! Do not lean over the battery when making this connection. *Important!* Do not allow the two cars to touch each other! Be sure all electrical equipment except the ignition is turned off on the car you are trying to start.

4. Now start the car with the good battery. Then start the car with the low battery. Disconnect the jumper cables. Disconnect the cable from the engine block first. Then disconnect the other end of this cable. Finally, disconnect the other cable.

5. Throw away the cloths used to cover the vent holes. They may have acid on them.

Note: Never crank the engine for more than 30 seconds at a time. Cranking longer may overheat and damage the starting motor.

10. TUNE UP

You should have a complete tune-up every 30,000 miles (48,000 km). During the tune-up, the technician will check the following items.
1. Ignition system and ignition timing.
2. Engine idle speed.
3. Clutch (if car has one).
4. Steering.
5. Suspension.
6. Exhaust system.
7. Brakes.
8. Fuel lines.
9. Throttle and transmission linkages.
10. Carburetor.
11. Emission controls.
12. Wheel bearings.
13. Front alignment.
14. Other items previously mentioned in this chapter, such as tires, fluid levels, cooling system, and battery. Also, the complete procedure includes chassis lubrication, changing engine oil, oil filter, and air-cleaner element; and installing new spark plugs.

Most service facilities have printed tune-up forms which list all the services that will be performed. Check this form to make sure that everything will be done. If no form is available, make a list of what is to be done so the technician can check off each service as it is performed.

11. FRONT-END ALIGNMENT AND WHEEL BALANCING

If you notice that your tires are wearing unevenly (pages 52 to 54), or you have a steering problem (car pulls to one side, wanders, or the front-end shimmy), you should have the front-alignment of your car checked and adjusted. Also, hard steering, rough riding, and abnormal tire wear can result if wheels are out of balance.

Many car owners have the wheel balance and front-alignment of their cars checked periodically. This helps to assure them of smooth riding and easy steering.

10-10   Balancing a wheel by placing a weight on the wheel rim. *(Bear Manufacturing Company)*

WHEEL BALANCE

Wheels can be balanced either on or off the car. A common method is to spin the wheel (either on or off the car) and notice whether or not it wobbles or is off center. Another method is to remove the wheel and put it in a static balancer. This device indicates whether the wheel is off balance.

The correction, if the wheel is out of balance, is to attach weights to the rim of the wheel (Fig. 10-10). This corrects the balance by counteracting the off center weight that caused the original out-of-balance conditions.

FRONT-END ALIGNMENT

The front wheels must roll true. That is, when the car is moving straight ahead, both wheels must point straight ahead. Also, they must be vertical to the road. In addition, the supports for the front wheels must tilt inward and backward somewhat. All these factors are important and contribute to good tire wear and easy steering.

There are various tests that the technician makes when checking front alignment. One measurement is to make sure the front wheels roll parallel to each other when the car is moving straight ahead. If they do not, an adjustment is made.

Another test measures the vertical alignment of the wheels with the road. The front wheels are given a slight outward tilt at the top to start with. Then, when the car is loaded and rolling forward on the road, the load will just about bring the wheels to vertical. This slight outward tilt is called positive camber.

A third measurement checks the backward tilt of the wheel support. This backward tilt is called positive caster. Its purpose is to help bring the wheels back to straight ahead after a turn.

Both camber and caster can be adjusted on most cars. The front alignment of the wheels can also be adjusted. Correct adjustment of these variable assures smooth steering and good tire life.

REFERENCES

If you are interested in learning more about the automobile, its construction, operation, and repair, you might like to refer to these books. Some are specialized and cover only one component, such as the engine. Others are more general and provide a survey of the complete car. You may find these books in your local library, or they may be ordered through a bookstore.

Automotive Air Conditioning, 2d ed., 1983, 292 pages. (Crouse and Anglin) McGraw-Hill Book Company. How and why automotive air conditioning systems work, their possible troubles, and comprehensive servicing of typical systems.

Automotive Body Repair and Refinishing, 1st ed., 1980, 378 pages. (Crouse and Anglin) McGraw-Hill Book Company. How car bodies are designed and constructed. Adjusting fit of doors, trunk lids, hoods. Repairing minor and major damage to the body or frame. Refinishing the body, including painting.

Automotive Brakes, Suspension, and Steering, 6th ed., 1983, 324 pages. (Crouse and Anglin) McGraw-Hill Book Company. Comprehensive treatment of brakes, suspension, and steering systems. How they work, possible troubles, servicing. Wheel alignment.

Automotive Emission Control, 3d ed., 1983, 278 pages. (Crouse and Anglin) McGraw-Hill Book Company. Sources of atmospheric pollution from automobiles. Controlling devices that reduce or prevent pollution. Their operation and servicing.

Automotive Engines, 6th ed., 1981, 422 pages. (Crouse and Anglin) McGraw-Hill Book Company. Comprehensive coverage of the various types of engines used in automobiles. Their construction, operation, possible troubles, servicing, and repair.

Automotive Electronics and Electrical Equipment, 9th ed., 1981, 360 pages. (Crouse) McGraw-Hill Book Company. Electronics in automobiles. Electrical equipment including starting, charging, and ignition systems. Troubles, servicing, and repair. Electronic fuel injection. Lights, horns, indicating devices.

Automotive Fuel, Lubricating, and Cooling Systems, 8th ed., 1981, 326 pages. (Crouse and Anglin) McGraw-Hill Book Company. Comprehensive coverage of these three vital systems and how they interrelate with the engine. Their operation, possible troubles, servicing, and repair.

Automotive Manual Transmission and Power Trains, 6th ed., 1983, 290 pages. (Crouse and Anglin) McGraw-Hill Book Company. Various types of manual transmissions, transaxles, and transfer cases. How they work, how they are constructed, their possible troubles, servicing, and repair. Power trains including drive line, joints, and differential.

Automotive Mechanics, 8th ed., 1980, 640 pages. (Crouse) Mc-Graw-Hill Book Company. Comprehensive coverage of all components of the automobile except body. The purpose, construction, operation, and servicing of each component is explained. Detailed trouble-diagnosis charts.

Automotive Tuneup, 2nd ed., 1983, 406 pages. (Crouse and Anglin) McGraw-Hill Book Company. Operation and servicing of all automotive components involved in tuneup, plus the complete tuneup procedure.

Automotive Technician's Handbook, 1st ed., 1979, 664 pages. (Crouse and Anglin) McGraw-Hill Book Company. Basic servicing procedures on all automotive components except body. This book is aimed at the person who is a practicing automotive mechanic or technician, or who wants to be.

Small Engine Mechanics, 1st ed., 1980, 362 pages. (Crouse and Anglin) McGraw-Hill Book Company. Detailed survey of small engines as used in lawn mowers, edgers, minibikes, snowblowers, chain saws, water pumps, air compressors, sprayers, grinders, post-hole diggers, and many other devices. Includes construction, operation, and servicing of small engines.

Motorcycle Mechanics, 1st ed., 1982, 360 pages. (Crouse and Anglin) McGraw-Hill Book Company. Comprehensive survey of all types of motorcycles and motorcycle engines, including construction, operation, troubleshooting, and service. Includes engines, fuel-lubricating, and ignition-systems, clutches, transmissions, final drives, frames, suspension, steering, brakes, wheels, and tires.

The Auto Book, 3rd ed., 1984, 628 pages. (Crouse and Anglin) McGraw-Hill Book Company. An introductory course in automotive mechanics, covering mainly the construction and operation of automotive components. Some servicing information.

GLOSSARY

The following glossary contains selected automotive terms and their definitions. Definitions are only partial. That is, they cover only what specifically applies to automotive service. The purpose of this glossary is to enable you to look up any automotive service term that puzzles you. For more complete coverage of automotive service terms, refer to the 118-page *Pocket Automotive Dictionary* (William H. Crouse, and Donald L. Anglin, McGraw-Hill Book Company, 1976). Also, all of the books listed in the Reference section have glossaries.

A

A. Abbreviation for **ampere**, a measure of electric current.

A/C. Abbreviation for **air conditioning**.

AC or ac. Abbreviation for **alternating current**.

accelerator. A foot-operated pedal, linked to the throttle valve in the carburetor; used to control the flow of air-fuel mixture to the engine.

accelerator pump. In the carburetor, a pump which momentarily enriches the air-fuel mixture when the accelerator is depressed at low speed.

additive. A chemical added to gasoline or oil to improve the gasoline or oil.

advance. The moving ahead of the ignition spark, produced by centrifugal or vacuum devices in accordance with engine speed and intake-manifold vacuum.

afterboil. Boiling of fuel in the carburetor or coolant in the engine cooling system immediately after the engine is stopped.

afterrunning. When an engine continues to run after the ignition is turned off. Sometimes called **dieseling**.

air bags. A passive restraint system with balloon-type passenger-safety devices that inflate automatically on vehicle impact.

air conditioning. An accessory system that cools, cleans, and dries passenger-compartment air.

air filter. A filter that removes dirt and dust particles from air passing through it.

air-injection system. An exhaust-emission control system that injects air into the exhaust manifold to complete the combustion of unburned hydrocarbons and carbon monoxide in the exhaust gas.

air pollution. Contamination of the air by natural and people-produced pollutants.

air resistance. The drag on a vehicle moving through the air. It increases as the square of vehicle speed.

air suspension. Any suspension system that uses air for vehicle springing.

alternating current. Electric current that flows first in one direction and then in the opposite direction.

alternator. In the vehicle electric system, a device that converts mechanical energy into electric energy for charging the battery and operating electrical accessories. Also called an ac **generator**.

ammeter. A meter for measuring the current (in amperes) flowing through an electric circuit.

antifreeze. A chemical that is added to the engine coolant to raise the coolant boiling point and lower its freezing point.

antiknock compound. An additive put into gasoline to suppress spark knock or detonation — usually a lead compound such as tetraethyl lead.

antiskid system. A system installed in the brake system to prevent wheel lockup during braking and, thus, to prevent skidding.

asbestos. A fiber material that is heat resistant used for brake linings, clutch facings, and gaskets. It is dangerous to breathe asbestos dust.

automatic choke. A choke that positions the choke valve automatically in relation to engine temperature.

automatic level control. A suspension system which takes care of variations in load in the rear of the car; positions the rear at a predesigned level regardless of load.

automatic transmission. A transmission in which gear ratios are selected automatically, eliminating the necessity of hand-shifting gears.

automotive air pollution. Evaporated and unburned fuel and other by-products of combustion which escape from a motor vehicle into the atmosphere; mainly carbon monoxide (CO), hydrocarbons (HC), nitrogen oxides (NO_x), sulfur oxides (SO_x), and particulates.

B

backfiring. Pre-explosion of the air-fuel which causes the explosion to pass back around the opened intake valve and through the intake manifold and carburetor. Also, the loud explosion of overly rich exhaust gas in the exhaust manifold, which exists through the muffler and tail pipe with a loud popping or banging noise.

ball bearing. An antifriction bearing with an inner race and an outer race, and one or more rows of balls between them.

ball joint. A flexible joint made up of a ball within a socket. It is used in front-suspension systems and some valve-train rocker arms.

battery. An electrochemical device for storing energy in chemical form which can be released as electricity; a group of electric cells connected together.

battery charge. Restoring chemical energy to a battery by supplying a electric current to it for a period of time.

BDC. Abbreviation for **bottom dead center.**

bead. That part of the tire which fits the rim; the bead is made of steel wires, wrapped and reinforced by the plies of the tires.

bearing. A part that supports a load, reducing the friction between moving parts.

belted-bias tire. A tire in which the plies are laid on the bias, crisscrossing each other, with a belt on top of them. The rubber tread is vulcanized on the belt and plies.

belted-radial tire. A tire in which the plies run parallel to each other and perpendicular to the tire bead. Belts running parallel to the tire bead are applied over plies.

bias-belted tire. Tire with two extra belts just under the tread; the cords in these belts are set at an angle, or bias.

bias-ply tire. A tire in which the plies are laid on the bias, criss-crossing each other at an angle of about 30° to 40°.

bleeding. A process by which air is removed from a hydraulic system (brake or power steering) by operating the system to work out the air.

blow-by. Leakage of compressed air-fuel mixture and burned gases (from combustion) past the piston rings into the crankcase.

blower. A supercharger or a diesel-engine intake-air compressor. Also, the fan motor in a heater or air-conditioning system.

body. On a vehicle, the assembly of sheet-metal sections, together with windows, doors, seats, and other parts, that encloses the passengers, engine, and other components.

bottom dead center. The piston position at the lower limit of its travel in the cylinder; when the cylinder volume is at its maximum.

brake. A device used to slow, stop, or hold a vehicle or mechanism.

brake drag. A light contact between brake linings and drums or disks when the brakes are not applied. The result is the car pulls; the brakes may burn up from the generated heat.

brake drum. A metal drum mounted on a car wheel to form the outer shell of the brake; the brake shoes press against the drum to slow or stop drum and wheel rotation for braking.

brake fade. A "fading out" of braking effectiveness; caused by overheating from excessively long and hard brake application, or by water reducing the friction between braking surfaces.

brake fluid. A special non-mineral-oil fluid used in the hydraulic braking system. It transmits pressure through a system of tubing known as the brake lines.

brake grab. A sudden increase in braking at a wheel; often caused by contaminated linings.

brake lining. A high-friction material, usually asbestos, attached to the brake shoe. The lining takes the wear when the shoe is pressed against the brake drum or disk.

brake shoes. In drum brakes, curved metal pieces lined with brake lining which are forced against the revolving drums to produce braking action. In disk brakes, flat metal pads with brake linings which are forced against the disk faces.

C

camber. The tilt of the top of the wheels from the vertical; when the tilt is outward, the chamber is positive.

camshaft. The shaft in the engine which has cams for operating the valve mechanisms. It is driven from the crankshaft by gears or sprockets and a toothed belt or chain.

carbon (C). A black deposit left on engine parts such as pistons, rings, and valves by the combustion of fuel.

carbon dioxide (CO_2). A colorless, odorless gas which results from complete combustion; usually considered harmless.

carbon monoxide (CO). A colorless, odorless, tasteless, poisonous gas which results from incomplete combustion. A pollutant contained in engine exhaust gas.

carburetion. The actions that take place in the carburetor; converting liquid fuel to vapor and mixing it with air to form a combustible mixture.

carburetor. The device in many engine fuel systems which mixes fuel with air and supplies the combustible mixture to the engine.

car lift. A piece of shop equipment that can lift an entire vehicle or, in some cases, one end of a vehicle.

caster. Tilting of the steering axis forward or backward to provide directional steering stability.

catalytic converter. A muffler-like device used in exhaust systems; it converts harmful exhaust gases into harmless gases by a chemical reaction between a catalyst and the pollutants.

centigrade. A thermometer scale on which water boils at 100° and freezes at 0°. The formula °C = 5/9 (°F − 32) converts Fahrenheit readings to centigrade (Celsius) readings.

centimeter (cm). A unit of linear measure in the metric system; equal to approximately 0.39 inches.

chassis. The assembly of mechanisms that make up the major operating part of the vehicle; usually assumed to include everything except the car body.

choke. In the carburetor, a device used when starting a cold engine; it "chokes" the air flow through the air horn, producing a partial vacuum in the air horn for greater fuel delivery and a richer mixture. Operates automatically on most cars.

circuit breaker. A protective device that opens an electric circuit to prevent damage when overheated by excess current flow.

clutch. A coupling device which engages and disengages the transmission from the engine. In an air-conditioning system, the device which engages and disengages the compressor shaft.

CO. See **carbon monoxide.**

CO_2. See **carbon dioxide.**

coil. In an automobile ignition system, a transformer used to step up the battery voltage to the high voltage required to fire the spark plugs.

coil spring. A spring made of an elastic metal such as steel, formed into a wire and wound into a coil.

cold-patching. A method of repairing a punctured tire or tube by cementing a thin rubber patch over the hole.

collapsible steering column. An energy-absorbing steering column designed to collapse if the driver is thrown into it by a severe collision.

combustion. Burning; fire produced by the proper combination of fuel and oxygen. In the engine, the rapid burning of the air-fuel mixture in the combustion chamber.

compression ignition. The ignition of fuel solely by the heat generated when air is compressed in the cylinder. This is the method of ignition used in the diesel engine.

compression ratio. The volume of the cylinder and combustion chamber when the piston is at BDC, divided by the volume when the piston is at TDC.

condenser. In the ignition system, a device connected across the contact points to reduce arcing by providing a storage place for electricity (electrons) as the contact points open. In an air-conditioning system, the radiator-like heat exchanger in which refrigerant vapor loses heat and condenses to a liquid.

connecting rod. In the engine, the rod that connects the crank on the crankshaft with the piston.

constant-velocity joint. Two universal joints arranged so their acceleration-deceleration effects cancel each other out. This results in an output drive-shaft speed that is always the same as the input drive-shaft speed, regardless of the angle of drive.

contact points. In some ignition systems, the stationary and the movable points in the distributor which open and close the ignition primary circuit.

coolant. The liquid mixture of about 50 per cent antifreeze and 50 per cent water which circulates in the cooling system to carry heat out of the engine.

cooling system. The system that removes heat from the engine by the forced circulation of coolant. It includes the water jackets, water pump, radiator, and thermostat.

corrosion. Chemical action that eats away a metal.

crankcase. The lower part of the engine in which the crankcase rotates; includes the lower section of the cylinder block and the oil pan.

crankcase breather. The opening or tube that allows air to enter and leave the crankcase to permit crankcase ventilation.

crankcase dilution. Dilution of the lubricating oil in the oil pan; resulting from liquid gasoline condensing from the blow-by in a cold engine and seeping down the cylinder walls.

crankcase ventilation. The circulation of air through the crankcase of a running engine to remove water, blow-by, and other vapors. This prevents oil dilution, contamination, sludge formation, and pressure buildup.

crankshaft. The main rotating shaft of the engine, with cranks to which the connecting rods are attached; converts up and down (reciprocating) motion into circular (rotary) motion.

curb weight. The weight of an empty vehicle without payload or driver but including standard equipment.

current. A flow of electrons, measured in amperes.

cycling-clutch system. An air conditioner in which the conditioned-air temperature is controlled by starting and stopping the compressor.

cylinder. The round tube-like opening in an engine cylinder block in which a piston moves up and down.

cylinder head. The part of the engine that covers and encloses the cylinders. It contains water jackets and, on I-head engines, the valves.

cylinder sleeve. A replaceable sleeve, or liner, cast or pressed into the cylinder block to form the cylinder bore.

D

defroster. The part of the car heater system which melts frost or ice on the inside or windshield.

dehumidify. To remove water vapor from the air. In an air conditioner, the air is dehumidified as it passes through the evaporator. Water condenses from the air onto the cool evaporator coils.

detonation. Commonly referred to as spark knock or **ping.** In the combustion chamber, an uncontrolled second explosion (after the spark occurs at the spark plug) with spontaneous combustion of the remaining compressed air-fuel mixture, resulting in a pinging noise.

diesel cycle. An engine operating cycle in which air is compressed, and fuel oil is injected into the compressed air at the end of the compression stroke. The heat produced by the compression ignites the fuel oil, eliminating the need for spark plugs or a separate ignition system. The action is called **compression ignition.**

diesel engine. An engine operating on the diesel cycle and burning oil instead of gasoline.

dieseling. A condition in which an automobile engine continues to run after the ignition is off. Caused by failure of the throttle valve to close completely and carbon deposits or hot spots in the combustion chamber.

differential. A gear assembly between axles that permits one wheel to turn at a different speed than the other, while transmitting power from the drive shaft to the wheel axles.

dipstick. See **oil-level indicator.**

direct current. Electric current that flows in one direction only.

directional signal. A device that flashes lights to indicate the direction in which the driver intends to turn.

disk brake. Brake in which brake pads, on a vise-like caliper, grip a revolving disk to slow or stop it.

displacement. The total volume of air-fuel mixture an engine is capable of drawing into all cylinders during one operating cycle.

distributor. In the ignition system, the rotary switch that directs high-voltage surges to the engine cylinders in the proper sequence. See **ignition distributor.**

driveability. The operating condition of an automobile, usually rated from good to poor; based on smoothness of idle, even acceleration, ease of starting, quick warm-up, and tendency to overheat at idle.

drive line. The connection between the transmission and the differential; made up of one or more drive shafts.

drive shaft. An assembly of one or two universal joints and slip joints connected to a metal tube; used to transmit power from the transmission to the differential. Also called the **propeller shaft.**

dry-charged battery. A new battery that has been charged, and then stored with the electrolyte removed. Electrolyte must be added to activate the battery when it is sold.

dynamometer. A device for measuring the power output of an engine.

E

electric brakes. A braking system with elelectromagnets at each wheel;

when the electromagnet is energized, it causes the brake shoes to move against the brake drum

electric current. A movement of electrons through a conductor such as a copper wire; measured in amperes.

electric system. In the automobile, the system that electrically cranks the engine for starting; furnishes high-voltage sparks to the engine cylinders to fire the compressed air-fuel charges; lights the lights; and powers the heater motor, radio, and other accessories. Consists, in part, of the starting motor, wiring, battery, alternator, regulator, ignition distributor, and ignition coil.

electronic fuel-injection system. A system that injects gasoline into a spark-ignition engine. It includes an electronic control to time and meter the fuel flow.

electronic ignition system. An ignition system which does not have mechanical contact points in the distributor, but uses the distributor for distributing the secondary voltage to the spark plugs.

electronic spark control. A system that controls the vacuum to the distributor, preventing vacuum advance below a selected vehicle speed.

engine. A device that burns fuel to produce mechanical power; sometimes referred to as a **power plant.**

engine tune-up. A procedure for inspecting, testing, and adjusting an engine, and replacing any worn parts, to restore the engine to good operating condition.

Environmental Protection Agency (EPA). The independent agency of the United States Government that sets standards and coordinates activities related to automotive emissions and the environment.

ethylene glycol. A widely used type of permanent antifreeze.

exhaust emissions. Pollutants emitted into the atmosphere from the engine.

exhaust gas. The burned and unburned gases that are left after combustion.

exhaust-gas analyzer. A device for sensing the amounts of air pollutants in the exhaust gas of a motor vehicles.

exhaust-gas recirculation system. An NO^x control system that recycles a small part of the exhaust gas back through the engine to lower the combustion temperature.

exhaust system. The system through which exhaust gases leave the vehicle. Consists of the exhaust manifold, exhaust pipe, muffler, catalytic converter, tail pipe, and resonator.

F

fan. The bladed device behind the radiator that rotates to draw cooling air through the radiator.

filter. A device through which air, gases, or liquids are passed to remove impurities.

firing order. The order in which the engine cylinders fire, or deliver their power strokes, starting with cylinder number one.

flat rate. Method of paying mechanics and technicians, using a manual which indicates the time normally required to do each service job.

flooded. This means that the engine cylinders have received raw or liquid gasoline, or an air-fuel mixture too rich to burn.

fluid coupling. A device in the power train consisting of two rotating members; transmits power from the engine, through a fluid, to the rest of the power train.

flywheel. A heavy metal wheel that is attached to the crankshaft and rotates with it. It helps smooth out the power surges from the engine power strokes. It also serves as part of the clutch (where used) and engine cranking system.

four on the floor. Slang for a four-speed transmission with the shift level mounted on the floor of the driving compartment.

four-wheel drive. A vehicle with driving axles at both front and rear, so that all four wheels can be driven.

frame. The assembly of metal structural parts and channel sections that supports the car engine and body and is supported by the wheels.

Freon-12. Refrigerant used in automobile air conditioners.

friction. The resistance to motion between two bodies in contact with each other.

front-end geometry. The angular relationship among the front wheels, wheel-attaching parts, and car frame. Includes camber, caster, steering-axis inclination, toe-in, and toe-out on turns.

front-wheel drive. A vehicle having its drive wheels located on the front axle.

fuel. Any combustible substance. In an automobile engine, the fuel (gasoline or oil) is burned, and the heat of combustion expands the resulting gases. This forces the piston downward and rotates the crankshaft.

fuel-injection system. A system which delivers fuel under pressure into the combustion chamber (diesel), or into the air flow before it enters the cylinders (spark-ignition).

fuel pump. The electrical or mechanical device in the fuel system which delivers fuel from the fuel tank to the carburetor.

fuel system. In a spark-ignition engine, the system that delivers the combustible mixture of vaporized fuel and air to the engine cylinders. Consists of the fuel tank and lines, gauge, fuel pump, carburetor, and intake manifold. In the diesel engine, the system that injects fuel oil into the engine cylinders.

fuel tank. The storage tank for fuel on the vehicle.

fuse. A device designed to open an electric circuit when the current is excessive, to protect equipment in the circuit. An open, or "blown", fuse must be replaced after the circuit problem is corrected.

fusible link. A type of fuse in which a special wire melts to open the circuit when the current is excessive. An open, or "blown", fusible link must be replaced after the circuit problem is corrected.

G

gear ratio. The number of revolutions of a driving gear required to turn a driven gear through one complete revolution. For a pair of gears, the ratio is found by dividing the number of teeth on the driven gear by the number of teeth on the driving gear.

gearshift. A linkage-type mechanism by which the gears in an automobile transmission are shifted.

glow plug. A plug-type heater containing a coil of resistance wire that is heated by electric current to warm the diesel engine precombustion chamber; for improving cold-engine starts.

grease. Lubricating oil to which thickening agents have been added.

H

hazard system. Also called the **emergency signal system**; a driver-controlled system of flashing front and rear lights, used to warn other motorists.

HC. Abbreviation for **hydrocarbon**.

headlights. Lights at the front of a vehicle designed to illuminate the road ahead of the vehicle.

heated-air system. A system in which a thermostatically controlled air cleaner supplies hot air from a stove around the exhaust manifold to the carburetor during warm-up; improves cold-engine operation.

heat of compression. Increase of temperature caused by the compression of air or air-fuel mixture.

hesitation. Momentary pause in the rate of acceleration; momentary lack of throttle response at some car speed.

high-compression. Term used to refer to the increased compression ratios of modern automotive engines.

high-voltage cables. The secondary (or spark-plug) cables or wires that carry high voltage from the ignition coil to the spark plugs.

hood. The part of the car body that fits over and protects the engine.

horn. An electrical noise-making device on a vehicle; used for signaling.

horsepower. A measure of mechanical power, or the rate at which work is done.

H_2O. Chemical symbol for hydrogen oxide, or water.

hot patching. A method of repairing a tire or tube by using heat to vulcanize a patch onto the damaged surface.

hub. The center part of a wheel.

hydraulic brakes. A braking system that uses hydraulic pressure to force the brake shoes against the brake drums or disks, as the brake pedal is depressed.

hydraulic clutch. A clutch that is actuated by hydraulic pressure.

hydraulics. The use of a liquid under pressure to transfer force or motion, or to increase an applied force.

hydrocarbon (HC). An organic compound containing only carbon and hydrogen. Gasoline is a blend of liquid hydrocarbons refined from crude oil.

hydrogen (H). A colorless, odorless, highly flammable gas whose combustion produces water. It is the simplest and lightest element.

I

idle. Engine speed when the accelerator pedal is fully released.

idle mixture. The air-fuel mixture supplied to the engine during idling.

idle-mixture adjustment screw. The adjustment screw (on some car-

117

buretors) that can be turned to adjust the idle mixture. Sealed in modern carburetors to prevent tampering.

idle system. In the carburetor, the passages through which fuel is fed when the engine is idling.

ignition. The action of the spark in starting the burning of the compressed air-fuel mixture in the combustion chamber.

ignition advance. The moving forward, in time, of the ignition spark relative to the piston position.

ignition coil. The ignition-system component that acts as a transformer to step up (increase) the battery voltage to many thousands of volts; the high-voltage surge from the coil is transmitted to the spark plug to ignite the compressed air-fuel mixture.

ignition distributor. The ignition-system component that closes and opens the primary circuit to the ignition coil (on contact-point systems) at the proper times and distributes the resulting high-voltage surges from the ignition coil to the proper spark plugs.

ignition switch. The switch in the ignition system (usually operated with a key) that opens and closes the ignition-coil primary circuit.

ignition system. In the automobile, the system that furnishes high-voltage sparks to the engine cylinders to fire the compressed air-fuel mixture. Consists of the battery, ignition coil, ignition distributor, electronic control, ignition switch, wiring, and spark plugs.

ignition timing. The timing of the spark at the spark plug.

independent front suspension. The front-suspension system in which each front wheel is independently supported by a spring.

insulation. Any substance that stops the travel of electricity (electrical insulation) or heat (heat insulation).

insulator. A poor conductor of electricity or of heat.

intake manifold. A device with passages through which the air-fuel mixture flows from the carburetor or injector to the ports in the cylinder head or cylinder block. In the diesel engine, only air flows through.

intake stroke. The piston stroke from TDC to BDC immediately following the exhaust stroke, during which the intake valve is open and the cylinder fills with air-fuel mixture.

K

kilogram (kg). In the metric system, a unit of weight and mass; approximately equal to 2.2 pound.

kilometer (km). In the metric system, a unit of linear measure; equal to 0.621 mi.

kilowatt (kW). A unit of power, equal to about 1.34 horse power.

kinetic energy. The energy of motion; the energy stored in a moving body through its momentum; for example, the kinetic energy stored in a moving car.

knock. A heavy metallic engine sound which varies with engine speed; usually caused by a loose or worn bearing. Name also used for detonation, pinging, and spark knock. See **detonation.**

kW. Abbreviation for **kilowatt.**

L

leaded gasoline. Gasoline to which small amounts of tetraethyl lead are added to reduce detonation.

leaf spring. A spring made up of a single flat steel plate, or several plates of graduated lengths assembled one on top of another; used on vehicles to absorb road shocks by bending, or flexing.

liquefied petroleum gas (LPG). A hydrocarbon for use as an engine fuel. It is a vapor at atmospheric pressure but becomes a liquid under sufficient pressure. Butane and propane are the liquefied gases most frequently used in automotive engines.

liter (l). In the metric system, a measure of volume; approximately equal to 0.26 gal (U.S.), or about 61 in^3. Used as a metric measure of engine-cylinder displacement.

lower beam. A headlight beam intended to illuminate the road ahead of the vehicle when meeting or following another vehicle.

LPG. Abbreviation for **liquefied petroleum gas.**

lubricating system. The system in the engine that supplies moving engine parts with lubricating oil.

M

manifold. A device with several inlet or outlet passageways through which a gas or liquid can flow. See **exhaust manifold, intake manifold.**

manifold vacuum. The vacuum in the intake manifold that develops as a result of the vacuum in the cylinders on their intake strokes.

master cylinder. In the hydraulic braking system the liquid-filled cylinder where the hydraulic pressure is developed when the driver depresses a foot pedal.

mph. Abbreviation for **miles per hour,** a unit of speed.

muffler. In the engine exhaust system, a device through which the exhaust gases must pass to reduce the exhaust noise.

N

needle bearing. An antifriction bearing of the roller type, in which the rollers are very small in diameter (needle-sized).

neutral. In a transmission, the setting in which all gears are disengaged.

nitrogen oxides (NO$_x$). Any chemical compound of nitrogen and oxygen. Nitrogen oxides result from high temperature and pressure in the combustion chambers of automobile engines during the combustion process. When combined with hydrocarbons in the presence of sunlight, nitrogen oxides form smog. A basic air pollutant; automotive exhaust-emission levels of nitrogen oxides are controlled by law.

NO$_x$. Abbreviation for any **nitrogen oxides.**

O

octane number. The number used to indicate the octane rating of a gasoline.

octane rating. A measure of the antiknock properties of a gasoline. The higher the octane rating, the more resistant the gasoline is to spark knock or detonation.

oil. A liquid lubricant; made from crude oil and used to provide lubrication between moving parts. In a diesel engine, oil is used for fuel.

oil filter. A filter which removes impurities from crankcase oil passing through it.

oil pan. The detachable lower part of the engine, made of sheet metal, which encloses the crankcase and acts as an oil reservoir.

oil pump. In the lubricating system, the device that delivers oil from the oil pan to the moving engine parts.

oil pumping. Leakage of oil past the piston rings and into the combustion chamber; usually the result of defective rings or worn cylinder walls.

oil ring. The lower ring or rings on a piston; designed to prevent excessive amounts of oil from working up the cylinder walls and into the combustion chamber. Also called an **oil-control ring.**

one-wire system. On automobiles, use of the car body, engine, and frame as a path for the grounded side of the electric circuits; eliminates the need for a second wire as a return path to the battery or alternator.

overcharging. Continued charging of a battery after it has reached the charged condition. This action damages the battery and shortens its life.

overdrive. In the transmission, an extra set of gears. They cause the drive shaft to overdrive, or drive faster than, the engine crankshaft; when engaged.

overhaul. To completely disassemble a unit, clean and inspect all parts, reassemble it with the original or new parts, and make all adjustments necessary for proper operation.

overhead-camshaft (OHC) engine. An engine in which the camshaft is mounted on the cylinder head, instead of inside the cylinder block.

overhead-valve (OHV) engine. An engine in which the valves are mounted in the cylinder head above the combustion chamber, instead of the cylinder block; in this type of engine, the camshaft can be mounted in the cylinder blockor on thecylinder-head.

P

parking brake. Mechanically operated brake that is independent of the foot-operated service brakes on the vehicle.

PCV valve. The valve that controls the flow of crankcase vapors in as required to ventilate the crankcase for different engine speeds and loads.

petroleum. The crude oil from which gasoline, lubricating oil, and other such products are refined.

photochemical smog. Smog caused by hydrocarbons and nitrogen oxides reacting photochemically in the atmosphere. Can cause eye and lung irritation.

ping. Engine "knock" that occurs only during acceleration. It may occur in higher speed ranges under heavy-load conditions. The cause is too much spark timing advance or low-octane fuel.

piston. In the engine, the cylindrical part that moves up and down within a cylinder to cause the crankshaft to rotates.

piston rings. Rings fitted into grooves in the piston. There are two types: compression rings for sealing the compression in the combustion chamber, and oil rings to scrape excessive oil off the cylinder wall. See **compression ring** and **oil ring.**

piston slap. A hollow, muffled, bell-like sound made by an excessively loose piston slapping the cylinder wall.

pitman arm. In the steering system, the arm that is connected between the steering-gear sector shaft and the steering linkage, or tie rod; it swings back and forth for steering as the steering wheel is turned.

pliers. Hand-held pincer-like tools used for cutting and gripping.

plies. The layers of cord in a tire casing, each of which is a ply.

pollutant. Any substance that adds to the pollution of the atmosphere. In a vehicle, any such substance in the exhaust gas from the engine, or evaporating from the fuel tank or carburetor.

positive crankcase ventilation (PCV). A crankcase ventilation system to return the crankcase vapors and blow-by gases from the crankcase to the engine to be burned. This prevents their escape into the atmosphere.

power. The rate at which work is done. A common power unit is the horsepower, which is equal to 33,000 ft-lb/min (foot-pounds per minute).

power brakes. A brake system that uses intake manifold vacuum to provide most of the effort required for braking.

power stroke. The piston stroke from TDC to BDC immediately following the compression stroke, during which both valves are closed and the air-fuel mixture burns, expands, and forces the piston down to turn the crankshaft.

power train. The mechanisms that carry the rotary motion developed in the engine to the car wheels; includes the clutch, (on some cars), transmission, drive shaft, differential and axles.

precombustion chamber. In most automotive diesel engines, a separate small combustion chamber into which the fuel is injected and where combustion begins.

preignition. Ignition of the air-fuel mixture in the combustion chamber before the ignition spark occurs at the spark plug.

prevention maintenance. The systematic inspection of a vehicle to detect and correct failures, either before they occur or before they develop into major defects.

propane. A type of LPG that is liquid below — 44°F (– 42°C) at atmospheric pressure.

propeller shaft. See **drive shaft.**

puncture-sealing tires or tubes. Tires or tubes coated on the inside with a plastic material. Air pressure in the tire or tube forces the material into a puncture; it hardens on contact with the air to seal the puncture.

Q

quick charger. A battery charger which produces a high charging current and thus substantially charges, or boosts, a battery in a short time.

R

rack-and-pinion steering gear. A steering gear in which a pinion on the end of the steering shaft meshes with a rack on the major cross member of the steering linkage.

radiator. In the cooling system, the device that removes heat from coolant passing through it. Hot coolant from the engine flows through it and returns to the engine at a lower temperature.

rear-end torque. The reaction on the rear-axle housing when torque is applied to the wheels. It tends to turn the axle housing in a direction opposite to wheel rotation.

recapping. Tire repair in which a cap of new tread material is vulcanized on the old casing.

recharging. The action of forcing electric current into a battery to reverse the chemical reaction that produced battery current.

Refrigerant-12. The refrigerant used in vehicle air-conditioning systems. It is sold under such trade names as Freon-12.

resistance. The opposition to a flow of current through a circuit or electrical device; measured in ohms.

rich mixture. An air-fuel mixture that has a relatively high proportion of fuel and a relatively low proportion of air. An air-fuel ratio of 13:1 is a rich mixture, compared to a lean air-fuel ratio of 18:1.

rivet. A fastener used to hold two pieces together.

roadability. The steering and handling qualities of a vehicle while it is being driven on the road.

rocker arm. In an I-head engine, a device that rocks on a shaft (or pivots on a stud) as the cam moves the pushrod, causing a valve to open.

rod bearing. In an engine, the bearing in the connecting rod in which a crankpin of the crankshaft rotates. Also called a **connecting-rod bearing.**

S

SAE. Abbreviation for **Society of Automotive Engineers.** Used to indicate a grade or weight of oil measured according to Society of Automotive Engineers standards.

screw. A metal fastener with threads that can be turned into a threaded hole. There are many different types and sizes of screws.

sealed-beam headlight. A headlight that contains the filament, reflector, and lens in a single sealed unit.

service manual. A book published annually by each vehicle manufacturer, listing the specifications and service procedures for each make and model of vehicle. Also called a **shop manual.**

shackle. The swinging support by which one end of a leaf spring is attached to the car frame.

shift lever. The lever used to change gears in a transmission. Also, the lever on the starting motor which moves the drive pinion into or out of mesh with the flywheel teeth.

shim. A strip of metal used as a spacer to adjust the front-end alignment on many cars; also used to make small corrections in the position of body sheet metal and other parts.

shimmy. Rapid oscillation. In wheel shimmy, for example, the front wheel turns in and out alternately and rapidly; this causes the front end of the car to oscillate, or shimmy.

shock absorber. A device placed at each vehicle wheel to control spring rebound and compression.

sight glass. In a car air conditioner, a viewing glass or window set in the refrigerant line, usually in the top of the receiver-dehydrator. It allows a visual check of the refrigerant passing through the system.

sludge. An accumulation of water, dirt, and oil in the oil pan; sludge is very viscous and can retard oil circulation.

smog. A term coined from the words **smoke** and **fog.** Describes any condition of dirty air and/or fumes or smoke. Smog is compounded from smoke, moisture, and pollutants produced by combustion.

spark knock. See **detonation.**

spark plug. A device that screws into the cylinder head of a spark-ignition engine provides a spark to ignite the compressed air-fuel mixture in the combustion chamber.

spring. A device that changes shape under stress or pressure, but returns to its original shape when the stress or pressure is removed.

stabilizer bar. An interconnecting shaft between the two lower suspension arms; reduces body roll on turns.

starting motor. The electric motor that cranks the engine, or spins the crankshaft, for starting.

steam cleaner. A machine used for cleaning large parts with a spray of steam, often mixed with soap.

steering-and-ignition lock. A device that locks the ignition switch in the Off position and at the same time locks the steering wheel so it cannot be turned.

steering gear. That part of the steering system that is located at the lower end of the steering shaft. It carries the rotary motion of the steering wheel to the car wheels for steering.

steering kickback. Sharp and rapid movements of the steering wheel as the front wheels encounter obstructions in the road; the shocks of these encounters "kick back" to the steering wheel.

steering knuckle. The front-wheel spindle which is supported by upper and lower ball joints. The part on which a front wheel is mounted, and which is turned for steering.

steering shaft. The shaft extending from the steering gear to the steering wheel.

steering system. The mechanism that enables the driver to turn the wheels and change the direction of vehicle movement.

steering wheel. The wheel, at the top of the steering shaft, which the driver uses to guide, or steer, the car.

stoplights. Lights, at the rear of a vehicle, which indicate that the brakes are being applied by the driver to slow or stop the vehicle.

storage battery. A device that changes chemical energy into electric energy. It stores electrical energy in chemical form.

streamlining. The shaping of a car body so that it minimizes air resistance and can be moved through the air with less energy.

stumble. The tendency of an engine to falter, and then catch, resulting in a noticeable hesitation. A momentary abrupt deceleration during an acceleration.

supercharger. In the intake system of the engine, a device that pressurizes the ingoing air-fuel mixture. This increases the amount of mixture delivered to the cylinders and thus increases the engine output. If the supercharger is driven by the engine exhaust gas, it is called a **turbocharger.**

surface ignition. Ignition of the air-fuel mixture, in the combustion, by hot metal surfaces or heated particles of carbon.

surge. Condition in which the engine speed increases and decreases slightly but perceptibly, even though the driver has not changed the throttle position.

suspension. The system of springs and other parts which supports the upper part of a vehicle on its axles and wheels.

sway bar. See **stabilizer bar.**

T

tachometer. A device for measuring engine speed, or revolutions per minute.

taillights. Steady-burning low-intensity lights used on the rear of the vehicle.

temperature gauge. A gauge that indicates, to the driver, the temperature of the coolant in the engine cooling system.

tetraethyl lead. A chemical which, when added to engine fuel, increases its octane rating, or reduces its knocking tendency. Also called **ethyl.**

thermometer. An instrument which measures heat.

thermostat. A device for the automatic regulation of temperature; usually contains a temperature-sensitive element that expands or contracts to allow or close off the flow of air, a gas, or a liquid.

throttle valve. A round disk valve in the throttle body of the carburetor; can be turned to admit more or less air, thereby controlling engine speed.

tie-rod end. A socket and a ball stud in the steering linkage. They rotate and tilt to transmit steeering action under all conditions.

tie rods. In the steering system, the rods that link the pitman arm to the steering-knuckle arms.

tilt steering wheel. A type of steering wheel that can be tilted to various angles, through a flex joint in the steering shaf .

timing. In an engine, delivery of the ignition spark or operation of the valves (in relation to the piston position) for the power stroke.

timing light. A light that can be connected to the ignition system to flash each time the number one spark plug fires; used for adjusting the timing of the ignition.

tire. The casing-and-tread assembly (with or without a tube) that is mounted on a car wheel to provide contact and traction with the road.

tire rotation. The interchanging of the locations of the tires on a car, to equalize tire wear.

tire tread. See **tread.**

tire tube. An inflatable rubber device mounted inside some tires to contain air at sufficient pressure to inflate the casing and support the vehicle weight.

tire-wear indicator. Small strips of rubber molded into the bottom of the tire tread grooves; they appear as narrow strips of smooth rubber across the tire when the tread depth decreases to 1/16 inch (1.59 mm).

toe-in. The amount, in inches or millimeters, by which the front wheeels point inward.

toe-out on turns. The difference between the angles each of the front wheels makes with the car frame, during turns. On a turn, the inner wheel turns, or toes out, more. Also called **steering geometry.**

top dead center (TDC). The piston position when the piston has reached the upper limit of its travel in the cylinder, and the center line of the connecting rod is parallel to the cylinder walls.

torque converter. In an automatic transmission, a fluid coupling which incorporates a stator to permit a torque increase.

torque wrench. A wrench that shows how much torque is being applied with the wrench.

torsion-bar spring. A long, straight bar that is fastened to the vehicle frame at one end and to a suspension part at the other. Spring action is produced by a twisting of the bar.

tracking. Rear wheels following directly behind (in the tracks of) the front wheels.

tramp. Up-and-down motion (hopping) of the front wheels at higher speeds, due to unbalanced wheels or excessive wheel runout. Also called **high-speed shimmy.**

transistor. An electronic device that can be used as an electric switch; is part of the electronic control unit in electronic ignition systems.

transmission. An assembly of gears that provides the different gear ratios, as well as neutral and reverse, through which engine power is transmitted to the drive shaft.

tread. The part of the tire that contacts the road. It is the thickest part of the tire, and has grooves to provide traction for driving and stopping.

trouble diagnosis. The detective work necessary to find the cause of a trouble.

tubeless tire. A tire that holds air without the use of a tube.

tune-up. A procedure for inspecting, testing, and adjusting an engine, and replacing any worn parts, to restore the engine to good operating condition.

turbocharger. A supercharger driven by the engine exhaust gas.

turbulence. The state of being violently disturbed. In the engine, the rapid swirling motion imparted to the air-fuel mixture entering a cylinder.

U

universal joint. In the power train, a jointed connection in the drive shaft that permits the driving angle to change.

unleaded gasoline. Gasoline to which no lead compounds have been added. Required by law to be used in vehicles equipped with catalytic converters.

upper beam. A headlight beam intended primarily for distant illumination, not for use when meeting or following other vehicles.

upshift. To shift a transmission into a higher gear.

unsprung weight. The weight of that part of the car which is not supported on springs; for example, the wheels and tires.

V

vacuum advance. The advancing (or retarding) of ignition timing by changes in intake-manifold vacuum, which reflect throttle opening and engine load.

vacuum gauge. A device that measures intake-manifold vacuum and thereby indicates actions of engine components.

vacuum switch. A switch that closes or opens its contacts in response to changing vacuum conditions.

valve. A device that can be opened or closed to allow or stop the flow of a liquid or gas.

valve clearance. The clearance in the valve train when the valve is closed.

valve grinding. Refacing a valve in a valve-refacing machine.

valve guide. A cylindrical part in the cylinder head in which a valve is assembled and in which it moves up and down.

valve lifter. A cylindrical part of the engine which rests on a cam of the camshaft and is lifted, by cam action, so that the valve is opened. Also called a **lifter, tappet, valve tappet,** or **cam follower.**

valve-refacing machine. A machine for removing material from the seating face of a valve to true up the face.

valve seat. The surface in the cylinder head against which a valve comes to rest to provide a seal against leakage.

vaporization. A change of state from liquid to vapor or gas, by evaporation or boiling.

vapor lock.   A condition in the fuel system in which gasoline vaporizes in the fuel line or fuel pump; bubbles of gasoline vapor restrict or prevent fuel delivery to the carburetor.

vibration damper.   A device attached to the crankshaft of an engine to oppose crankshaft torsional vibration (that is, the twist-untwist actions of the crankshaft caused by the cylinder firing impulses). Also called a **harmonic balancer.**

viscosity.   The resistance to flow exhibited by a liquid. A thick oil has greater viscosity than a thin oil.

viscosity rating.   An indicator of the viscosity of engine oil. There are separate ratings for winter driving and for summer driving. The winter grades are SAE5W, SAE10W, and SAE20W. The summer grades are SAE20, SAE30, SAE40, and SAE50. Many oils have multiple-viscosity ratings, as, for example SAE10W-30.

volatility.   A measure of the ease with which a liquid vaporizes.

voltage.   The force which causes electrons to flow in a conductor. The difference in electrical pressure (or potential) between two points in a circuit.

vulcanizing.   A process of treating raw rubber with heat and pressure; the treatment forms the rubber and gives it toughness and flexibility.

W

Wankel engine.   A rotary engine in which a three-lobe rotor turns eccentrically in an oval chamber to produce power.

water jackets.   The spaces between the inner and outer shells of the cylinder block or head, through which coolant circulates.

water pump.   The device in the cooling system that circulates coolant between the engine water jackets and the radiator.

wheel alignment.   Tests and adjustments to ensure that wheels and tires are properly aligned on the vehicle.

wheel balancer.   A device that checks a wheel-and-tire assembly for balance.

wheelbase.   The distance between the center lines of the front and rear axles.

wheel cylinders.   In a hydraulic braking system, hydraulic cylinders located in the brake mechanisms at the wheels. Hydraulic pressure from the master cylinder causes the wheel cylinders to move the brake shoes into contact with the brake drums or disks for braking.

wheel tramp.   Tendency for a wheel to move up and down so it repeatedly bears down hard, or "tramps", on the road.

window regulator.   A device for opening and closing window; operated by a crank or an electric device.

windshield wiper.   A mechanism which moves a rubber blade back and forth to wipe the windshield; operated either by intake manifold vacuum or electrically.

wiring harness.   A group of individually insulated wires, wrapped together to form a neat, easily installed bundle.

INDEX